Lynda Field is a trained counsellor, life coach and psychotherapist who specialises in personal and group development. She is the author of many best-selling titles, including *Weekend Life Coach, 60 Ways to Feel Amazing* and *60 Ways to Change Your Life*. In addition to giving seminars and workshops worldwide, she runs a telephone and on-line coaching service, and writes articles for a variety of national magazines. She lives in Essex, UK.

Visit Lynda on-line at: www.weekendlifecoach.com or email her at lyndafield@weekendlifecoach.com

D0928525

✶ ✩ ✶

*Dedicated to Barbara Higham,
my own personal Angel!*

✶ ✩ ✶

INTRODUCTION

Life coaching is fast becoming recognised as one of the most popular and effective approaches to bringing about real life transformations. And I know that there are so many of you who would love to take the opportunities to change that coaching offers. It's all a question of finding the time, isn't it?

I have written this little book for all of you who are trying to get your life together on the run! Yes, you *can* find the time to go for your goals and reach for your dreams, however busy you are.

Instant Life Coach slips easily into your handbag or briefcase so that you can dip into it at any free moment throughout your day. Whenever you feel the need for a shot of inspiration just try one of these 200 life-coaching tips and start to turn your life around.

Instant Life Coach is packed with easy and practical ways to bring positive energy into all aspects of your life; so why not start today to make your dreams come true?

With all my very best wishes

Lynda Field

RESPOND CREATIVELY

The only way to change your circumstances is to change yourself and you have been born with the capacity to do this: use this ability. When life throws us a challenge we have three choices:

Dive for cover and look for a scapegoat.

Become the scapegoat.

Respond creatively.

Looking for and being the scapegoat are the choices of the victim (likes to be a martyr; feels non-deserving; has low self-worth; doesn't want any responsibility; can always blame others; is afraid to rock the boat; never has to take a risk).

Responding creatively is the choice of someone who knows they have the power to make positive changes. This response is not always easy and it requires courage and tenacity at a time when things might be very difficult. But what else have we to do in this life if not to take responsibility for ourselves and the way that we live?

Victim consciousness is always linked with low self-esteem. How could we continue to let ourselves: lose out; miss out; get treated like a doormat; be abused and the rest, unless we believed that we deserved to be treated in this way? When you next find yourself diving for cover or flirting dangerously with guilt and blame ask yourself these questions: Where is my self-respect? What do I deserve? Am I a person with integrity? How can I stand up for myself? Am I taking responsibility for my life?

Take your life into your own hands and respond creatively.

BELIEVE IN YOURSELF

Self-confident people have indestructible self-belief, nothing can take away their feeling of self-worth and they bounce back again and again. You can feel like this. You have all that it takes to go for what you want and to ride the ups and downs that life inevitably brings. No one has a smooth trip but just think how you will feel if you don't even give yourself a chance to get out there and give things a try!

Self-belief checklist

A person with self-belief:

◆ Never compares herself with others.

◆ Knows that she is her own woman and that nobody else can understand her as well as she can.

◆ Listens to helpful advice and comments but never blindly follows others' opinions.

◆ Trusts her instincts and listens to her heart.

- ◆ Recognises that she will make mistakes and learns from them and moves on.
- ◆ Depends upon her own judgement and always gives herself time to work things through.
- ◆ Values rest and relaxation as much as action planning and activity.
- ◆ Knows that when she is calm and focused she will make the best decisions.
- ◆ Accepts that there will be days when her self-belief is not so strong and will wait until she is feeling more positive before committing herself to any course of action.

☆ ☆ ☆

When you are high in self-belief you will trust your own thoughts and feelings and will be able to follow through with appropriate action.

SIMPLIFY YOUR LIFE

If our lives are cluttered with material objects we feel psychologically crowded, with no space to think and relax. We can bring order out of chaos by simplifying the way that we live and this leads to an increase in mental clarity and lowers our stress levels.

An ancient universal law states that to bring more abundance into our lives we first have to create room to allow ourselves to receive this new prosperity. Whilst we hang on to the redundant and useless articles that surround us we are metaphysically hanging on to old energy patterns and past limitations.

Take that closet full of clothes for example. Why are you keeping items that you never wear and know for sure that you will never wear again?

Check out your sentimental attachment to that old skirt/coat/bag, etc. And why are you keeping that dress that was always too small for you? Every time you look at clothes that don't fit you and never will, you will always undermine your body confidence (it's enough to make you reach for the biscuit tin).

Don't let the past hold you back – if you haven't worn something for the last three years, bin it! How can we welcome the new and the good if we have nowhere to put it?

Let go of the old and welcome the new.

– 4 –

MAKE SOMETHING HAPPEN

What is the difference between people who make things happen and those who just seem to have things happen to them? Why can one person create new directions for herself whilst another always seems to be the victim of circumstances? The difference lies in their ability to make decisions.

How do you feel about making decisions? Would you describe your decision-making powers as:

Good?

Not so good?

Poor?

Can't decide?

When we are not feeling our best our self-respect plummets and it becomes very hard to trust our own judgement. One way to overcome this is to use a rather clever strategy. IDA is a simple formula that you can use whenever you are uncertain about what to decide and therefore how to act. IDA represents the following process:

INTENTION ➜ DECISION ➜ ACTION

You can't act if you can't decide how to act, and you can't make a decision unless you know what you intend to happen. Discover your intention by asking yourself, 'What do I want to happen?' Then decide how you need to change your behaviour. Then change your behaviour by acting differently.

When you know what you want you will make things happen.

– 5 –

DISCOVER YOUR POSITIVE AND NEGATIVE INFLUENCES

EXERCISE

You are what you believe you are

Write down 20 words that best describe you.

1 . . . .   2 . . . .

3 . . . .   4 . . . .

5 . . . .   6 . . . .

7 . . . .   8 . . . .

9 . . . .   10 . . . .

11 . . . .   12 . . . .

13 . . . .   14 . . . .

15 . . . .   16 . . . .

17 . . . .   18 . . . .

19 . . . .   20 . . . .

Look at your answers one at a time and decide
which beliefs have **P**ositive implications for you and
which have **N**egative associations.

Put an **N** or a **P** next to each word.

Now go back and consider each of your **N**
answers. Think carefully about why you believe
these things to be true. Each time ask yourself, 'Is
this really true?'

Challenge your negative beliefs;
why believe something that
doesn't work for you?

– 6 –

KEEP YOUR COOL

Think of a time when your emotions ran away with you. Did you say what you wanted to say? Did you act the way you wanted to act? Did you get the result you wanted? The answers were probably 'no'. It's hard to remain clear and in control when you are feeling hot and bothered. Here is a brilliant exercise that will cool you out. Try it before you laugh at it; it really works!

EXERCISE

The emotion cooler

1 Put your right thumb over your right nostril, just lightly closing it off.

2 Exhale. Inhale slowly through your left nostril only for twenty complete breaths. Keep your mouth closed all the time. Make the breaths as long and smooth as you can. Each time you exhale let go of all tension, hurt, anger, irritability and any other negative emotions.

Visualise these emotions draining out of your body so that you feel clear and positive.

3 You may have to excuse yourself for a few moments to do this. It's very useful during a heated telephone discussion when it is possible to do it without being detected.

Research shows that physiological and psychological states are reflected in the way that we breathe. By controlling which nostril is functioning we can tune into the different hemispheres of the brain. When we breathe through our left nostril we are connecting with the right side of our brain, which controls our receptive, spiritual and inner awareness.

Try it now, before the heat is on, and feel the difference in your relaxation levels.

SAVE MONEY

Ten easy ways to save

1 When you experience that must-have urge, stop and count to ten slowly. Then ask yourself, 'Do I really need this?' And if you are still blinded by desire ask yourself, 'Can I afford this?' Both cruel but crucial questions.

2 Instead of eating out with your friends why not have them round to your place for a simple meal, and let them bring the wine and pudding.

3 Wait until the sales to do your clothes shopping; you will get some great bargains.

4 Resist hire purchase agreements (very costly). It's worth saving up for that big item until you can pay for it with cash, when you will pay far less.

5 Check out upmarket second-hand 'nearly new' shops that sell designer

clothes for a fraction of their original cost.

6 Eat before you go supermarket food shopping. And while you are there keep an eye open for 'Bogofs', as in Buy One Get One Free.

7 If you are spending £5 a day on a sandwich and drinks that adds up to £100 a month. Take your own lunch to work and you will save over half of what you were spending.

8 Work out your budget for daily expenditures and stick to it!

9 Join a library and order the books you would otherwise have to buy. Check out the DVDs, CDs and videos too.

10 Save regularly and treat this as an essential payment.

Get into some good shopping habits and watch your savings grow.

— 8 —

NURTURE YOURSELF
FOR A DAY

What does it mean to nurture yourself?

Do you nurture yourself?

How do you treat yourself?

Think of the way you would treat a small helpless child. You would feed her if she was hungry and comfort her if she was crying. If she made a mistake you would forgive her and if she fell over you would pick her up and help her back on her feet. You would encourage her in every way you knew. She is free to make mistakes because this is how she learns. You know that this child will develop through love and support and that she will not develop and learn if she is criticised.

Now answer the following questions.

◆ Do you treat yourself in this caring way?

- ◆ Do you love and encourage yourself?
- ◆ Do you help yourself up when you fall and comfort yourself when you are sad?
- ◆ Do you forgive yourself when you make a mistake?

We find it so difficult to treat ourselves in this loving and nurturing way. Decide to nurture yourself for a day and see how it goes. Say the following affirmation to yourself throughout the day.

AFFIRMATION:

I deserve love and care.

Try to make sure that every thought or action of the day is one that supports and encourages you. Remember how you would treat that small child? Well, treat yourself in exactly the same way.

Nurture yourself for a day and the habit may grow.

FIND YOUR WORK/LIFE BALANCE

The pressure of having to keep everything together (by throwing and catching all those balls) can often feel just too much. If this sounds like you, it's time to reassess and get your life into perspective. Put *your* health and well-being first; if you burn out the game is over. Try the following tips to help you create a happier and more balanced lifestyle.

Eight tips for balancing work and home

1 Prioritise yourself! Schedule free time for doing nothing, even if you are surrounded by chaos.

2 Learn to settle for a less than perfect home. Domestic jobs just keep on coming; accept this and stop trying to always keep on top.

3 Delegate household tasks, make a

list of jobs for everyone and make sure they do them. This is as easy as it sounds. (I've done it and it works a treat.)

4 Book some exercise time into your diary, but don't take your foreign language tapes with you to the gym (practise doing one thing at a time).

5 Look at the bigger picture of your life: you are meant for greater things than meeting all those targets.

6 Take time to stand and stare; practise this and you will find the habit will grow on you.

7 When you just can't beat the clock remember your sense of humour. Laughter brings things back into perspective.

8 Slow down your breathing, your talking, your pace.

Take time to appreciate your precious life.

SAVE TIME

In life coaching we talk about the 80/20 rule, which helps to remind us to make good choices about where to put our time and energy. This rule says that 20 per cent of your activities will be likely to create 80 per cent of the significant achievements in your life.

Save time:

◆ on minor tasks and spend it on more valuable activities. Get into the habit of *writing down* your top daily priorities and keep checking this list to ensure that you are dealing with them.

◆ on procrastinating and spend time getting on with it!

◆ on dwelling on your inadequacies, and spend time concentrating on your strengths.

◆ trying to be perfect and spend the extra time you gain doing something entirely relaxing and self-indulgent (scented bath, sauna, facial, swim, sleep… you name it!).

◆ on worrying, and spend it on problem solving.

◆ thinking about your self-doubts, and spend it on your positive self-beliefs.

◆ by always acting with awareness so that you won't have to pay for your mistakes in the future.

◆ wondering what people are thinking about you, and spend it on pleasing yourself.

◆ dwelling on the past and worrying about the future, and spend it making a go of it now!

◆ believing that life can't be fun, and spend it believing that it can be.

Spend your time where it matters most.

27

SCREAM YOUR HEAD OFF

It has been a difficult day. Everyone was late getting up and you had to rush to get the children to school; then you were late for work and realised you had left an important file at home; then the tea machine stopped working; then the babysitter phoned to say she couldn't make it tonight, and then...

Whatever particular sequences of events or people have come together to create tension in your life, how are you going to cope with it?

We all know what it feels like to be tense, and when we feel it we are certainly not at our rational best. Tension inevitably leads to explosion, often inappropriate explosion. The person you finally scream at has usually had absolutely nothing to do with the small stress-inducing items that have built up to create your volcano of anger. Before you reach the point of explosion try the following strategy.

Silent screaming

Go and find a quiet and private spot.

Stretch your mouth as wide as you can and tense your facial, neck and head muscles. The rest of your body might feel pretty tense too.

Then, clench your fists and beat the air and scream ... silently!

Relax totally and repeat once again. Do this until you feel better. You may even find yourself moved to laughter!

Let go of stress as quickly as you can; it lowers your ability to take control of your life.

− 12 −

FEEL YOUR FEELINGS

Our feelings are important but sometimes we deny them because we are afraid of what people might think of us. Have you ever done this?

Our society does not encourage us to express our feelings, and men usually have even more trouble than women in this area. How many men do you know who are able to talk about their emotions? You may well have had a close relationship with someone who has denied their feelings for so long that they don't even know what they are feeling any more.

It is very common for me to ask a client how they are feeling and for them to reply that they 'don't know'. People who are out of touch with their emotions are not being true to themselves and will inevitably be low in self-esteem.

Check your feelings

Give yourself some 'feeling checks' throughout the day.

Whenever you remember, stop for a moment and ask yourself, 'What am I feeling right now?'

Before you make an important decision just consider your true feelings. What do you really *feel* would be the right thing to do?

When it's difficult to decide (you can't sort out your feelings) take a rain check and let yourself sleep on it. Our emotions have a very neat way of sorting themselves out as we sleep and often we can wake up with a new creative solution.

When you recognise your feelings you are recognising your needs.

– 13 –

FALL IN LOVE WITH YOUR GOALS

One of the easiest ways to get things done efficiently and enjoyably is to start to think differently about any task that you are doing.

Think of a job that needs doing – now how do you feel? Are you delighted and energised by the prospect or do you feel pressurised and stressed? Can you feel your energy levels going up or going down?

It's not hard to see that the more delighted you feel to do something, the more likely it is that you will be able to accomplish it in a relaxed, focused and efficient way. Notice what happens when you say to yourself, 'I've got to do this' or 'I should do that' or 'I must do the other'; your energy drops through the floor and you feel reluctant and unwilling to get going. This is when you can come up with all those reasons not to do something (too busy, too tired, no time).

Now, if you turn your attitude around and say to yourself, 'I'm glad to do this' you will discover a new spring in your step. Create an eager mood and you will find yourself invigorated by a fresh new wave of 'can do' energy. I tell my clients to fall in love with their goals and this is such a terrific tip. Get passionate about them, keep thinking how wonderful they are, adore the prospect of achieving them, and the rest is easy.

Love your goals and
enliven your energy.

TAKE A LEAP OF FAITH

Significant changes always involve risk-taking and if you are looking for a major change in lifestyle then you must be prepared to take a leap of faith. This is how you do it.

You must be committed; there can be no half-measures. If you think you *might like* a new job or getting fit *sounds like a good idea* or it *might be nice* to move house or start a new relationship or *you should* or *ought to* stop smoking, change your job...then you can just forget it. You *must* be moved by a passionate desire in order to provide the forceful impulse which will trigger the energy needed to create the change.

You must feel the fear and do it anyway. Change is a risky business and it is fear of taking risks that has held you back until now. You might be afraid that you will look a fool, or that others might reject you, or that you are bound to fail. You need to know that *everyone* who has ever done anything meaningful in their lives has had to face and overcome their own inhibiting demons. The most amazing things happen when you decide to believe in yourself: others start to demonstrate their belief in you. As soon as you are prepared to move that one step forward, invisible forces will give you the strength to make a quantum leap. Try it!

Believe in yourself and
take that leap.

CELEBRATE YOUR ALONENESS

You are unique. There is no such thing as a normal or average size or type of person. Everyone is absolutely special and individual. When we recognise our uniqueness we also recognise our aloneness. Sometimes our aloneness can be very scary. We may feel lonely because no one can ever really understand how we feel and always be there for us. It is true that no one will ever know the inner you. You are the only person who can know yourself. No one else can be inside you. And would you really want anyone to know everything about you?

This idea of our aloneness carries a wonderful quality of freedom. We can release our expectations of other people to know all about us and we can stop feeling guilty about not always being there for others.

Frightening or freeing – your aloneness

can be either of these things. Choose freedom; choose to celebrate your alone-ness. Repeat the following affirmation, which will help you to accept and enjoy the inevitability of feeling alone.

AFFIRMATION:

I am sitting on top of the world and I belong to nobody and nobody belongs to me.

As you say this affirmation use your imag-ination to visualise yourself at the top of the world feeling free. Feel the freedom that comes with these words.

When we are truly free to be ourselves all our relationships improve and we feel wonderful.

– 16 –

TAKE THE JOYFUL PATH

Imagine this: you are standing at an intersection and one route is the path to struggle and one is the path to joy. You can choose which to take.

Joy and struggle are not the result of things happening to you, they are attitudes; filters; approaches; frameworks, and you are always free to choose.

- ◆ Why come from fear when you can come from love?

- ◆ Why look at the mud when you can look at the stars?

- ◆ Why expect the worst when you can expect the best?

- ◆ Why choose to be a victim when you can create your own realities?

- ◆ Why be miserable when you can be happy?

Give up the struggle, just for today. Just for today try the path of joy. Suspend all disbelief, fear and cynicism and let joy into your life. Take your joyful consciousness out into the world and smile. Stay in the moment, no dwelling in past problems or future fears and keep looking for the joyful path. When someone complains, recognise the path of struggle. If someone treats you badly, don't join them on their path; turn the other cheek. Don't be distracted by the emotions and actions of others; keep in your calm and joyful centre. Do this for one day and see how it works. Don't be trapped by your thoughts and fears, choose to be uplifted instead. Every time you radiate joy you attract it back to you in even greater measure.

One joyful day might just lead to another.

ENJOY YOUR WORK

We take ourselves wherever we go and we cannot escape our own beliefs, attitudes, expectations and moods. It's so easy to blame 'work' for our shortfalls (underachievement; lack of money; boredom); if we act like a victim at work we can expect to be treated like one.

It is always hard to succeed at anything if you don't enjoy it and maybe you don't like the work you do.

Take a creative approach to your dilemma. If you are unfulfilled and feeling resentful is there any way you can turn this around by changing your attitude? For example, if your salary supports you or your family perhaps you can find a sense of gratitude and appreciation for that.

When you can love your work (for whatever reason) the energy will start moving again and you will begin to attract new opportunities: positive energy always attracts more of the same.

And if you are fed up with work because you are longing for a different career, what are you doing to make this change happen? Do you need more training? Are you actively seeking new prospects? Are you networking and sending out copies of your résumé?

Act creatively and assertively to bring about positive changes.

Enjoy your work and you will enjoy your life.

GET GOING

Give yourself a boost of confidence by trying this simple tip.

Think of all the small jobs that you keep promising yourself that you will do (no great projects here, just those modest tasks that you just don't ever seem to get round to). Choose things like: clean out that drawer, write a letter to ..., phone ..., sew a button on my skirt, re-pot that plant ..., etc.

Make a list of these minor jobs.

Things I need to do

....

....

....

Make sure that you *do* write them down because they will become much more real and do-able. Never mind how long the list is. Now choose *one thing* from your list and do it. Now don't you feel great?

Sometimes, when we promise that we will get something together and then don't, we can slip into a negative cycle of low self-respect (feeling like we can't trust ourselves to follow through with *anything*). We often spend more time and energy thinking about doing something, and then not doing it, and then not liking ourselves for not doing it, than it would take to actually do it.

Break this habit and show yourself how easy it is to just do one of your overdue jobs and you will instantly move into a positively inspired cycle.

Next time you hear yourself saying, 'I really need to . . .' just go ahead and do it!

TAKE THE STRESS OUT OF YOUR JOB

It's all the rage to be stressed, but stress always lies in the eye of the beholder. When life at work starts getting to you, don't let yourself become a 'stress victim' who blames your job for all your negative mental states. Use a Positive Mental Approach to deal with difficult work scenarios and keep your mood upbeat and friendly. And remember, if after all this effort you are still feeling pressurised, it might be worth considering a career change!

Ten ways to be happy at work

1 Stop using the 'stress' label. If work life is troublesome understand the difficulties and then try to resolve them.

2 Be specific about the problems and name them; it then becomes easier to find solutions.

3 Discuss your situation with a trusted

friend; constructive feedback might bring new insights.

4 Don't moan or gossip; this path leads to a negative place.

5 Use good communication skills to express your needs assertively.

6 Don't let yourself be victimised by others. Whenever you act like a victim, others will treat you like one.

7 Think of your work problems as 'challenges' which you can overcome.

8 Use a creative approach to problem solving.

9 Keep positive and confident and people will treat you with respect.

10 Take your spirituality to the workplace. Use your intuitive awareness and natural empathy and you will be amazed by the way that others respond.

Take the stress out of work with a Positive Mental Attitude.

LISTEN FOR A DAY

Experience a day in a new way. Spend a day listening to everyone you meet rather than talking to them. Such an approach will change the whole focus of your day and will take you 'outside' yourself. It is easy to forget to listen because it's not something that we are very conscious of in our society. Indeed, listening has become a dying art.

Whenever we listen to people we are showing them that we value them and that we are interested in them and this appreciation encourages them to feel good about themselves. Your friends, loved ones and colleagues will respond fabulously to the increased attention and will have plenty to say and you will have time to hear it.

The 'feeling good' benefits exist for everyone involved in the communications. The people you listen to feel valued and respected. The good feelings will be returned and you will feel that you have done a good job and so your own self-esteem will rise.

Who is your favourite person, the one who you turn to when things get rough? What are the qualities that make this person so understanding? Do they include the ability to listen? I expect they do. Think of a time when someone really listened to you with every part of their being. How did you feel?

We learn so much about ourselves by listening to others; give it a try.

APPRECIATE YOUR TEAM

Do you know who is in your team? I'm not referring to the local football team here but to any group of people who work and co-operate with you. Teamwork and team-building are buzz words in the world of work because, of course, employers want people who can co-operate and communicate effectively with others. However, such important personal skills will enhance the performance of any group. You might belong to any number of teams: your work team, your family, parent group at school, darts club, sports club, drama group ... there are numerous possibilities. Make a list of all your teams.

My teams are

....

....

....

Good teamwork involves commitment, shared goals, support for other members and good interpersonal skills. Being part of a team increases our sense of belonging and well-being, and there is nothing quite like that shared feeling of a team achievement.

Increasing your team effort

- Think about your own teams and consider ways that you could increase your team effort.

- Are there ways where you could bring more to any of the groups that you are involved with?

- Do you share your strengths and abilities with other team members?

- Do you show your appreciation for those who live, work and play with you?

Appreciate your team and just notice the positive effect on its overall performance.

– 22 –

CHECK YOUR BODY CONFIDENCE

A top magazine recently commissioned a survey of 5,000 women and the overall conclusion drawn from the results was that we do not think that big is beautiful; in other words our size does matter. Eight out of ten women think about their shape every day (how many times a day, I wonder?), and more than eighty per cent feel inhibited by their body.

Yet another major survey demonstrates that most of us are suffering with what could be called the Bridget Jones Syndrome. In other words, we lack body confidence and are constantly preoccupied with the way that we look. A staggering ninety per cent of the 3,000 women taking part in the survey said that the appearance of their body depressed them, and one in ten admitted to being on a 'constant' diet.

Body confidence test

Answer the following questions and discover just how you really feel about your body.

- Do you feel physically strong and powerful?

- Do you hate any part of your body?

- Would you say that you are obsessed by the food you eat/don't eat?

- Do you feel free to enjoy eating?

- Do you weigh yourself more than twice a week?

- Do you think that you would be happier if you lost weight?

- Are you ever embarrassed by your body?

- Do you compare yourself with others?

- Do you think that looks are more important than skills and abilities?

You are gorgeous just the way you are — believe this!

KEEP YOUNG AT HEART

While my granddaughter longs to be a 'big girl', her mother (my daughter) is reminiscing about her own childhood. But we can have both the freedom of adulthood and the joys of childhood if we remain young at heart. Fun people can be any age – staying young is an attitude, it has nothing to do with how old we are.

Get in touch with some of your childhood memories. We all have memories of sensual experiences that link us to our past. They may be smells, tastes, textures, noises, movements ... Childhood memories can be rekindled by the touch of velvet, the taste of an aniseed ball, the smell of the sea, the sound of a church bell, a ride on a swing ...

EXERCISE

Revisit your childhood

Are there any sensual experiences that take you back to your childhood? Can you fill in any of the categories below?

Touch

Taste

Smell

Sound . . . .

Movement . . . .

If you have discovered any experiences that remind you of your childhood then *recreate that experience*. Go and eat a sherbet dip, watch *Peter Pan*, ride a donkey, blow some bubbles, sit on a hay bale, go to the fair and smell the candyfloss, and even eat it! Your list may start very small but as you pursue these memories you will open the floodgates of your childhood experiences. As you bite into that toffee apple you *are* the child within you.

Allow your inner child to play
and dance through life and you
will stay forever young.

SLAY ENERGY VAMPIRES

It's not always our activity that makes us tired. Sometimes we exhaust ourselves simply by letting people or circumstances drain away our energy.

Can you think of anything that might be demanding of you or distracting you or getting on your nerves at the moment? Are there any so-called *energy vampires* in your life? If there are you will know who and what they are.

Do you have to 'put up' with anything or anybody that annoys you and stops you moving forward in the important areas of your life? Such energy drainers could include: any domestic appliances that aren't working properly, unfinished work projects, an over-demanding acquaintance, broken toilet seats, dirty clothes continually dumped on the floor, a negative family member, an unreliable co-worker, a disorganised desk ...(you name them).

Make a list of your annoyances (petty and not so petty).

Now take your top three irritations, choose one and decide to do something about it.

Go back to your list; prioritise the items (most annoying at the top) and start to deal with them on a regular basis. When new possible distractions develop, just add them to your list. You will feel so much better because you will know that they are under control and that they will be dealt with soon.

Keep your energy strong and focused by dealing with energy vampires.

25

FORGIVE SOMEONE

Forgiveness is a powerful way of increasing our own feelings of self-worth and confidence. When I first suggest to people that they might forgive someone who angers them they usually say something like, 'Why should I after what they did to me?'

Forgiveness does not mean that we think that it's OK for anybody to do anything to us. Forgiveness is all about letting go. If I cannot forgive you, then my angry thoughts will connect me to you forever. You may live ten thousand miles away, but if all I have to do is think of you for my emotions to get stirred up then I might as well be living with you. We might even carry anger for a person who is dead. This is not at all unusual.

Is there anyone who you find difficult to forgive? If so, ask yourself what you gain from not forgiving this person. You gain a permanent relationship with the object of your hatred; you are bound together in anger. Is this what you really want?

Forgiving does not mean overlooking; it means the opposite. Before you can let go of the ties that bind you to another in hatred, you need to know exactly what hurt you and why and then to express this in an appropriate way.

When you can truly forgive you set yourself free.

How can you be high in self-esteem if you hate someone?

26

GET HIM TALKING

It is important to remember that, although most women are able to talk about their feelings as they are experiencing them, many men cannot do this! Accept that men and women are different in this respect and adopt a strategic approach that will encourage him to open up.

EXERCISE

Getting men to talk

Don't make statements such as: *You never tell me how you feel* or *Why don't we talk more?* or even *Why don't we plan some time to talk?* These might be interpreted as criticism and will close down the lines of communication immediately.

Organise talk time. Create some time in your busy schedules where you can be intimate and attentive. Be subtle, recreate your early dating days and give him your full attention (men love this). Ask him about his activities; this can lead to greater things. Don't expect too much at once.

Let him talk. And once he starts chatting, *let him talk!* Resist all temptation to empathise with him. Women fall automatically into 'overlapping' mode when they talk to each other. Your friend discloses a problem and you say something like 'I know exactly what you are going through'. We do this with each other to show support and it brings us closer together. Beware; *men hate this technique.* Resist the temptation to jump in there or he will close up and it will be you who is doing all the talking (again).

Learn to listen well and leave some spaces for him to talk into.

27

FEEL MORE CONFIDENT

Twenty ways to increase your confidence:

1 Smile!

2 Always expect the best.

3 Say what you mean.

4 Network – get out there and get noticed.

5 Look for the silver lining.

6 Learn something new – stretch yourself in some way and see how flexible you can be.

7 Break an old habit that you have outgrown.

8 Keep your sense of humour.

9 Find time to meet up with your friends regularly.

10 Allocate yourself regular 'me' time, because you are worth it!

11 Stop moving goalposts and celebrate any and every step along your way.

12 Spend time with someone who is a positive influence on you.

13 Remember that everything changes and bad times will pass.

14 Keep at it; don't give up on yourself.

15 Don't blow things out of proportion – don't sweat the small stuff!

16 Buy a great pair of shoes and then plan a special occasion to wear them.

17 Take a step towards one of your goals.

18 Repeat this mantra: *I deserve the best*. You do of course!

19 Take some exercise: you will feel like a new woman – move that body, even a short walk will do it.

20 Remember your strengths and demonstrate them.

Believe in yourself, trust yourself, have confidence in yourself.

28

MOVE YOUR BODY

Does the very thought of exercise propel you towards the sofa?

Sitting around all day can be very tiring whilst even moderate activity is actually an energising experience. As the blood starts pumping faster through your body you use up calories, tone your muscles, increase your feel-good endorphin and oxygen levels, and release anti-stress hormones into your bloodstream – plenty of reasons to get up off that sofa!

But you know all this already; the fact that exercise is 'good' for us is not enough to send us out for a jog; off to the gym; to the pool; or even out for a walk. We like our prizes instantly and the start of a fitness regime (however modest) will stretch us as we push that body to new limits; the rewards do come quite quickly however. Many studies have shown that there is a direct relationship between exercise and a positive mood (and we all know what positivity can do!).

We are often put off exercise because we make unrealistic plans for ourselves. If you want a beautifully toned and sculpted body you will have to put in the time, but you don't have to spend hours in the gym to become fit and less stressed. If you start your fitness regime in a small way (e.g. walking to work instead of taking the bus) you will find that your modest achievements will develop your inclination to create new fitness goals.

Move that body and feel the stress drop away.

29

BE YOUR OWN BEST FRIEND

So many clients tell me how much they hate themselves when they are feeling low in self-esteem. They criticise themselves for their behaviour, for mistakes they have made and for their inability to make decisions. When we are low in self-respect this self-hate just serves to take us even lower.

We can only break out of this negative trap when we are ready to be less hard and judgemental about ourselves. The way to increase our confidence always lies in a positive, upbeat and non-self-critical approach.

Next time you are feeling down try this wonderful technique, which can lift your mood so that you feel lighter and brighter and better about yourself.

Be your own best friend

Become your own best friend. Imagine that you
have stepped out of your body and that you are now
standing next to yourself. (Don't think too much
about this, just use your imagination.) Now look at
yourself.

- What can you say that is comforting and
  helpful?

- How can you encourage this person to feel
  more confident about herself?

- What would you say if it were your best friend
  standing there?

Perhaps you would put your arm around her and tell
her that she's doing really well and that you
appreciate all her good qualities. Talk to yourself
the way you would to your very closest friend.

*Become your own best friend
and your self-esteem will
immediately increase.*

30

INCREASE YOUR PERSONAL POWER

When we are high in personal power we are:

Confident   Decisive

Imaginative   Energetic

Purposeful   Effective

Focused   Centred

How often do you feel like this?

The concept of power is often linked with ideas of struggle, authority and conflict. I am using the word quite differently here. Your power is your own. It belongs to you and no one can change it, take it away or give you more. You create your own personal power or not as the case may be.

Whenever we start blaming external forces or other people for the things that happen to us, we give away our personal power.

Examples

After being given a poor seat in a restaurant: *'It's not fair, I never get given a good seat.'*

Working late for the third night in a row: *'My boss never thinks that I might have something better to do.'*

And whenever we wait for someone to change their behaviour we are giving away our power.

If you are waiting for someone to change you will wait forever. Every time you play the victim you give away your power to your victimiser. If it's someone else's fault then you can't do anything to change your situation. Take charge of your life: say 'no' when you need to, express your true feelings and don't let people treat you like a doormat.

Let go of blame, increase your personal power and be free to live your life dynamically.

31

GET IN TOUCH WITH YOUR OWN TRUTH

Life is all about change, and as we develop and grow we are playing a part in this natural process. You know how this works. Think of a time in the past when you were happy with a certain aspect of your life (relationship, job or whatever), and then your feelings changed and somehow things just didn't feel right any more. Your dissatisfaction was a sign that you had outgrown this particular situation and were ready to move on. We change continually and what was perfect last year (or even last week) might be far from perfect now. Be ready to look into your own eyes and to make a realistic assessment of where you are now. If you are feeling less than satisfied then this is a clear sign that something needs to change. Ask yourself some big questions and let your answers be big! Be expansive, express your real needs and desires and get in touch with your own truth.

Looking into your own eyes

Now ask yourself these questions:

- What do I really want to do with my life?

- What gifts do I bring?

- How can I develop my unique skills and strengths?

- Can I trust myself, and if not, why not?

- What are my greatest fears when I think about making changes?

- What is the first step I need to take to get myself moving again?

Let your dissatisfaction be
a sign to you that it is time
to take stock, reassess
and move on.

32

GET THE RESULTS YOU WANT

Next time you are sitting on the Tube or on a bus or even walking down a street, just take a close look at the people around you. Notice their energy (you can see and feel this very easily). Are they light and optimistic? Do they look happy and alert? Are they glowing with interest and spark? Do they meet your eyes when you glance at them?

You will see that the majority of people are preoccupied with their thoughts, and by the look of them those thoughts are not very optimistic. And here lies a vital point: positive people get the results they want because they believe in themselves and they believe in life. You have the power to turn around any negative state of mind and this will unlock your amazing creative potential. Are you ready to stand out and be different from the mainstream? Are you ready to attract success?

Ten ways to attract success

1 Be true to yourself.
2 Celebrate your uniqueness, this is what makes you special.
3 Develop your inner strengths and talents.
4 Think big.
5 Believe in yourself and radiate confidence.
6 Take the first step towards one of your goals.
7 Appreciate the miracle of your life.
8 Love and value all your experiences.
9 Be a go-getter.
10 Never ever give up!

Believe in yourself and be a success.

– 33 –

OPEN THE DOOR TO PROSPERITY

As soon as you become aware of your money habits (spending, saving and squandering) you can take immediate positive steps towards having more money.

Set some financial goals for yourself and don't expect too much too soon or you might be tempted to blow all your good intentions. Some realistic and useful short-term goals might include: to keep a money diary; stick to a realistic budget; stop impulse buying and to work on increasing your feelings of prosperity. Your long-term goals might be to take financial advice; increase your earnings; save for a big item and become more relaxed about money issues.

Don't ever forget that the key to your prosperity lies in your attitude. Think rich, let go of worries and negative beliefs about money and welcome feelings of abundance into your life; work on your positive beliefs and step out of scarcity consciousness. As soon as you do this you will find that you will want to get to grips with the ins and outs of your financial affairs.

Take control of your money issues and believe that you deserve to be rich and you will open the door to a life of abundance and prosperity.

When you take charge of your finances you will feel greatly empowered.

STOP BEING VICTIMISED

Are you being victimised? This might sound like an odd question as it can bring to mind such issues as bullying, hate mail or even physical violence. But we can become a victim to others in many subtle as well as not so subtle ways. Unwittingly, we can live our lives the way we do *because* of other people and unless we are continually checking out our feelings about 'why we do the things we do', we will remain in blissful ignorance of our victim status.

When do you stop being a good friend and start to become a victim? When do you stop becoming a good parent and slip into being victimised by your children?

Where is that point when your conscientiousness at work becomes burdensome to you and you feel taken for granted?

If you are feeling: guilty; irritated; low in self-esteem; impatient; muddled and confused around a particular person and/or situation, then you are allowing yourself to be victimised.

A victim is a person who gives away her power to other people. She is unconsciously creating realities in her life (relationships, experiences, situations, dilemmas) that reflect her negative beliefs, and she blames her discontent on others; she is a loser. A non-victim knows that she is responsible for the quality of her own life; she maintains a positive outlook and thereby attracts the best possible circumstances, relationships and lifestyle. She consciously creates her life by using positive affirmations and visualisations, and she is a winner!

You have the power
to be a winner.

- 35 -

YOU CAN WORK IT OUT

When you are troubled and don't know how to act, where do you turn? If you can't make a difficult decision, whom do you ask? When your life is a mess and you need to make changes, how do you start? Who is always there for you, in the bad times as well as the good? Who knows your weaknesses and strengths and can offer wise counsel at any time of the day or night? Who is it who will never let you down?

When the problems pile up we often forget that we have the inner strength and power to overcome any adversity. Sometimes it can feel that life is a maze of difficulties and that we can never find the way out – but we can. We possess incredible instinctive powers, but we usually fail to use them because we are no longer taught to value our intuitive gifts.

How many times have you looked back at a situation which has gone badly and thought, *I knew that would happen; I sensed I should have done this, that or the other; I should have listened to my intuition*?

The only person who can always be there for you is of course yourself: you can always find the way out of any dilemma.

Believe and know that you have access to all the answers to your problems. You possess all the inner wisdom you need; use it!

You have all the answers you need.

36

CHANGE YOUR NEGATIVE SELF-BELIEFS

When you look in the mirror, what sort of person do you see? This is a hard thing to do, especially on a day when we are not feeling so bright. We are so self-critical; we treat ourselves badly and can find so many things 'wrong' with ourselves.

Most of our negative self-beliefs have absolutely no foundation in reality. We are not really *selfish, unkind, cruel, lazy, thoughtless, stupid, no good, worthless* …etc. (I am sure that you can add your own personal favourites to this list). We learned our beliefs about ourselves at a very early age when we believed literally everything that we heard.

If, for example, I was told that I was stupid when I was very small, I may still hold that belief even now. I may be very clever, but deep down if I believe that I am stupid then I will always feel 'not good enough'.

We change our negative self-beliefs by training our minds to believe positive things instead. It really is very simple. For example, instead of continuing to believe that 'I am stupid' (which keeps me low in self-esteem) I will contradict this belief by making the following positive affirmation.

AFFIRMATION

I am intelligent

Make a positive affirmation for yourself. Just contradict any negative self-belief and repeat your affirmation as many times as you can remember to. Sing it, write it, say it under your breath and fill your mind with positivity.

Keep at it and eventually your positive affirmation will replace your negative belief.

37

CARPE DIEM – SEIZE THE DAY

This is it! This is another valuable moment of your precious life. This is not a dress rehearsal for the real thing; this *is* the performance of your life! Are you enjoying it?

Your life is a precious gift, miraculous and amazing, but you will not always be able to appreciate this miracle fully. Our difficulties and defeats cloud our vision and so we often lose sight of the glory of it all. Look at a newborn baby; see the wonder in its eyes. You can still see the world in this way; that baby hasn't gone anywhere, she just grew up.

EXERCISE

Things I would have to do

If you were told that you had four weeks to live, what would you do immediately? What would you want to say to whom? What unfinished business would you be taking care of? Make a list of all the important things that you would feel you had to do.

....

....

....

....

We are not immortal although we often live our lives as if we were. Embrace the day, live it wholeheartedly and do what you know you really need to do. Live it with passion, give it all you've got and just see what it gives back to you.

Take a look at the world as if you only have four weeks left – it looks different, doesn't it?

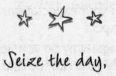

Seize the day,
today.

38

REACH YOUR FULL POTENTIAL

The ways that we restrict and limit our-selves are not always easy to detect because they are locked into our belief systems. Look at the following checklist to discover any of the ways that you might be restricting your own potential.

Checklist: Ways in which you might be limiting yourself

Low expectations: you get what you expect. What do you expect for yourself? What do you think you deserve? Circumstances and people walk through the doors of your expectations so watch what you expect.

Glass ceilings: why do you believe that you can only go so far; be that good; achieve only this much? You are the only person standing in your way.

Belief in scarcity: prosperity and

abundance abounds. Nature is prolific; love is everywhere; we are all connected in the most profound way; we are all here to cooperate with each other. Embrace abundance, love and trust and your glass ceilings will melt away.

Unhealthy boundaries: your boundaries delineate your sense of self and good, productive relationships depend on knowing where you stand and where you draw your lines in the sand. You cannot have a good relationship until you know yourself, so get your boundaries sorted.

Reluctance to change: whenever we feel threatened we naturally try to protect ourselves and so often we resist any change that exposes us to something new. But don't take this too far. Check: Is this change good for me? Why am I fearful? Are my fears realistic or unrealistic?

Allow yourself to be your best.

– 39 –

BE PERSISTENT

This is the quality of winners. Successful people never ever give up. There may be obstacles, disappointments and challenges along the way (especially if you are going for some really big changes) and you must be ready to face them.

Persistence is not a matter of keeping on doing the same thing even if it doesn't work. No, persistence is hitting a brick wall and realising that you must find a way over it, around it, through it, under it (or even maybe blow it up!). Winners look for creative solutions to their setbacks and they keep on trying alternatives until they find one that works.

When the going gets rough the tough just increase their self-belief and their determination to win through.

◆ Cultivate an image of yourself as a person who is a survivor who will always bounce back from any circumstance.

- Overcome the first hurdle and know that you are determined to succeed, and then go on to overcome the next hurdle.

- Celebrate every step along the way towards your goal and let each one serve to strengthen your resolve.

- Action makes you feel courageous; keep moving forward and your self-belief will go through the roof.

Whenever you strive to reach your potential you are acting like a winner; you cannot fail, whatever happens!

40

LEARN LIFE'S LESSONS

Think of your life as a training course that begins at birth and ends when you leave the planet. The modules of this course come in the form of personal challenges (problems, discontent, relationship hassles … etc.) and we are here to learn from these modules. If we don't learn from our lessons we have to repeat that part of the course.

For example, let's imagine that I am attracted to men who victimise me in some way. The lesson for me is *to recognise* that I keep choosing the wrong sort of man, *to understand* why I do this and then *to change* my behaviour. If I don't learn this lesson the module will be repeated (I will fall for the wrong man again). When I finally grasp this module I will have learned a lot about myself and about the type of love interest I would like to attract.

And so each learning experience brings more awareness and balance into our lives. But there is never an end to the learning and when we have learned something new and assimilated its meaning we move on to the next module.

You are a work in progress. You are here to learn life's lessons and they will never stop until your life ends. Accept this. Recognise that your life is an ongoing process of self-awareness and that the very nature of life (moving in cycles) ensures that you will continually experience ups and downs.

Recognise your lessons, understand what you need to learn and then change your behaviour accordingly.

41

REMEMBER THESE IMPORTANT THINGS

- Dreams can come true – believe in them.
- We are all connected.
- How to say what you mean – life will be a breeze.
- The more you give, the more you will receive.
- Expect the best – you get what you expect.
- You create your own reality.
- Forgiveness creates happiness – decide to let go.
- You are divine!
- Everyone is doing the best they can.
- How to say 'no' – you will stop being a victim.
- Every cloud has a silver lining.

- Everything changes – bad times will pass.
- Your life has meaning and purpose.
- How to accept a compliment – smile and say thanks.
- The universe supports you.
- Persistence pays – don't take no for an answer.
- You are incredible.
- How to smile dazzlingly – it will light up your life.

Take time each day to remember at least one of these things and you will feel the benefits.

42

HAVE NO REGRETS

Have you ever had any of these thoughts?

If only I had not done that.

I wish I had said something else.

I should have behaved differently.

I regret doing that.

If only I could do it all over again.

How could I have behaved so stupidly?

Such thoughts often come to us in the small hours of the morning when we have time to ponder our difficulties. We have all lain awake in the dark, worrying and blaming ourselves for what has happened and wishing that we had done something different.

Yes, we can all look back and regret our actions but *we cannot change the past*, and if we continue to agonise over what we should and shouldn't have done our lives will be miserable and we will be low in self-confidence. When past regrets are dominating your life you will feel stuck, de-motivated and unable to feel positive about anything. When you feel like this it's time to **let go of the past**.

EXERCISE

Let go of the past

1 Take an incident that is worrying you.

2 Look at it coolly and objectively.

3 Recognise that what's done is done.

4 Consider if there is anything you can do to remedy the situation.

5 If so then do it, and if not then *let go of it!*

You did the best you could at the time and now look forward to a positive future.

43

CREATE A SUCCESS LIST

When we are feeling low in self-esteem it is difficult to like anything about ourselves. When we are caught in a negative spiral of:

self-dislike ➜ feelings of powerlessness
➜ inability to make decisions ➜
inability to act ➜ self-dislike

There is a way to stop the rot. Clients often say how much they hate themselves. If I ask them to tell me about any positive things that they have experienced in their lives they find it very difficult to begin. One way to lift ourselves out of this negative cycle is to think about what we have done well in the past. *Maybe things don't look so good now, but what sort of achievements have we already made in our lives?*

I ask clients to create a 'success list'. This is a list of *everything* you are successful at, or have been a success at some time in your life. Include all areas of your life: relationships, work and leisure. What about coming first in the sack race on sports day? Do you remember learning to ride a bike? How about getting your first job? Going on your first date. Starting school. Passing your driving test. Go back as far as you can, make a fun thing of it, get a really big piece of paper and keep adding to the list. Memories of success will change your mood. Look at your list, what an incredible set of experiences!

You see, you aren't powerless, helpless and indecisive after all — you are a SUCCESS!

44

ACCEPT YOURSELF

Sometimes when things don't look so great we might start wishing that we were someone else or somewhere else! If only: I could get away from here; I had another job; I could meet a new lover; I had more money; I was more like ... Yes, the grass may look greener on the other side, but when you eventually get there you discover an obvious but amazing truth: you have taken yourself with you! There is no escaping yourself; changing your circumstances will not necessarily make you happier.

Contentment begins with self-awareness and self-acceptance and it focuses on the 'now'. Whilst you are wishing that things could be different you will always feel dissatisfied with what you have and who you are at this moment. The trick is to be able to accept yourself *just as you are* (including all the bits you don't like very much). When you are feeling more comfortable with who you are you gain a sense of inner peace and you take that with you wherever you go.

Success can be measured in many ways but we cannot define it by external criteria alone. True success is felt inside: it is an inner sense of satisfaction about a job well done; an opportunity grasped; an outcome achieved; a problem resolved; and it always brings with it an underlying feeling of appreciation and well-being.

Be yourself, accept yourself and appreciate yourself; you are fabulous!

45

GET LUCKY

If you radiate happy-go-lucky, light-hearted energy you lift the spirits of others around you and before you know it they are responding in a more upbeat way. There is no doubt that lucky people see the positive potential in everything, and this is a fabulous gift that you can give to yourself.

EXERCISE

See the positive potential

Lucky people even use bad luck to their advantage; they see the positive potential in *everything* that happens to them. The following exercise shows you how you can do this yourself.

- Things could be worse, just think of those who are in a more terrible situation.

- Get things in perspective by looking at the bigger picture. However bad it looks, know that 'this too will pass'.

- Remember the lucky breaks that you have

had in the past; expect one now.

- Every cloud has a silver lining; look for it.
- Learn from past mistakes and find new and creative ways to solve your problems.
- If bad luck strikes don't assume that you are powerless. List your options and look for a solution.

Lucky people look on the bright side of life and make the most of all their experiences (the good as well as the bad). Open yourself to the charms of Lady Luck; expect the best and do all that you can to achieve it and you will find new energy, excitement and motivation in everything you do.

Act lucky today; you have
everything to gain.

46

RISE TO YOUR CHALLENGES

You are here to reach for the stars, to realise your potential, to grow in self-awareness and to share your developing consciousness with others. When you are doing this you will feel centred, purposeful and fully alive and nothing can hold you back. Your life will become positive and meaningful when you stop complaining about your 'problems' and see them instead as 'challenges' that you will overcome. This is an entirely new take on the way that most people view their lives: the old moaning, problematic style doesn't work and never will; let it go.

EXERCISE

Rising to the challenge

- Bring to mind an ongoing problem, one that seems to keep popping up (your energy has probably already dropped at the mere thought of it).

- Write a brief factual description of the issues involved.

- Now decide to take a fresh look at this by keeping your energy upbeat and viewing your 'problem' as a 'challenge'.

- Notice how the different terms extract a different energetic response from you.

The word 'problem' brings images of obstacles and limitations (no wonder we feel so tired at the very mention of the word). However, we can rise to and overcome a challenge. So can you rise to this particular challenge of yours? Once you become aware of why you are attracting a particular challenge you can change your behaviour so that you can move on.

There is nothing standing in your way that you cannot step over.

47

DON'T SWEAT THE SMALL STUFF

As we rush around spinning all our plates and trying to find the time to relax it's easy to start to take life ultra-seriously. When this happens our irritation levels shoot sky high and before we know it we are feeling annoyed and upset at the slightest incident.

When you next find yourself getting wound up over something just stop and ask yourself this question: 'Does it really matter?' If it really does then get to grips with what must be done (appropriate action is a fine antidote to stress).

However, very often we allow ourselves to become worked up about something that really doesn't matter, and then our irritation can quickly lead us into negativity and feelings of low self-esteem.

Your daughter has dropped chocolate on her dress; your partner didn't stack the dishwasher properly; the house isn't perfectly tidy; a work colleague didn't do the task you asked her to do in *exactly* the way you would have preferred it to be done. Is it worth making a point? Is it worth getting upset?

When we are feeling good about ourselves these minor details are unimportant. When we are feeling low the small things really seem to matter.

The next time you feel your stress levels rising:

Ask yourself, 'Does it really matter?'

If the answer is no then remind yourself that this isn't important and that it's not worth getting upset over.

Let it go and move on.

Let go of minor irritations and
keep your stress levels down.

48

LAUGH YOURSELF SILLY

How do you feel when you have had a really good laugh? You feel great, don't you?

Laughing and smiling actually have amazing health-giving effects.

As you laugh you exercise your belly area and diaphragm.

This abdominal movement deepens your breathing which increases the oxygen flow into your body and improves your circulation.

Laughing expands blood vessels, which encourages tissue healing.

Smiling and laughing stimulates the production of endorphins (your body's natural painkillers), which produce a natural high.

When you laugh you are helping your lymphatic system to get rid of bodily wastes, you burn off fat and relax your muscles.

'Laughter is the best medicine.' You can't have a really good laugh and be anxious and stressed at the same time.

When you see the funny side of life you are more able to put things in perspective.

It's easier to ask yourself if your problem really matters that much.

What incredible benefits! However fed up you feel it surely is worth trying to find something to laugh about. Start with a smile, a smile can start to change your mood. Seek out something that has made you laugh in the past, a video, a book, the company of a certain friend, an activity...

Put a smile on your face and go for laughter, it can only make you feel one hundred per cent better.

49

GIVE YOURSELF SOME TLC

We can be unbelievably hard on ourselves, can't we? Just when we need some support and kindness we often generate its opposite: we become our own worst critics (unforgiving, intolerant and unkind). Self-criticism is a fast track to negativity, depression and dissatisfaction; don't take this route. When the chips are down search for some self-compassion; look for self-forgiveness; give yourself some tender loving care. Don't think that you are all alone with your negative self-beliefs. We all find it hard to become the person we would most like to live with. But practice makes perfect and you can start right now.

Forgive yourself

So, you have nasty thoughts and feel uncomfortable emotions; so do we all. Unless you are a saint you will share the whole range of human emotional responses and these are quite natural.

The next time you feel an uncomfortable emotion (such as jealousy, anger, shame or grief) don't compound it with guilt (because you 'shouldn't' be feeling it). If you feel it then you feel it.

Accept it and then it will pass; tie it up with guilt and you will stay locked within its jaws.

Start to notice when these 'unacceptable' emotions emerge and acknowledge and release them.

Forgive yourself and be kind to yourself and watch your life improve.

50

TALK YOURSELF UP

With positive self-talk you can 'talk yourself up' and lift your mental, emotional and spiritual energies; this naturally leads to the type of focused and effective action that accomplishes goals. In this way you can programme yourself to meet your challenges and also increase the belief that you can and will achieve whatever it is you are attempting to do. Try talking yourself up with the following positive, motivational statements.

I am determined and motivated and nothing stops me.

I feel great and ready for anything.

I love life and life loves me back.

Today I am on top of the world; anything is possible.

I go for my goals and I reach them; nothing stands in my way.

I am not afraid of anyone or anything; I feel confident and assertive.

Today I start my fabulous new life.

I believe in myself 100% and I am now ready to live my dreams.

I never make excuses; I do things on time and keep to my word.

I am so lucky to be alive.

Repeat these statements out loud. Don't worry if you don't believe that they are true, the bigger the 'lie' you feel you are telling, the more powerfully the statement will be affecting your negative beliefs. Notice how your energy changes when you make these upbeat declarations. Do they make you feel good? Say them again and again and again ...

Keep motivated.

51

STOP DOING

There is always so much to *do*, isn't there? How can we find the time for not doing and just *being*? A long time ago someone said to me, 'If you can't find time for yourself how can you expect anyone else to find time for you?' This stopped me in my ever-so-busy tracks and put me on a new road.

Find the time, you are worth it! Take a piece of paper and set out a weekly plan which shows when you will have time alone in order to *do* nothing and to *be* something. Even if you can only manage ten minutes a day this will be enough.

Dedicate this time to *being*. Sit quietly and alone, turn off all electronic distractions and close your eyes in the silence. Expect nothing, just experience yourself. If you have never done this before it can be quite a shock: noises, feelings, thoughts (especially thoughts) are calling for your attention and ten minutes can feel like hours. Stick at this, learn to ignore your internal chatter (it never stops so just let it go). This ten minutes a day is dedicated to *being*. Do this for a week and make a note of what happens and how you feel.

.Get used to time alone just doing nothing and you will find yourself feeling more relaxed and at ease.

☆ ☆ ☆

We are called human beings for good reason.

52

DON'T GO THROUGH THE WRONG DOORS

Have you ever tormented yourself with such unanswerable questions as:

- ◆ Why do I always get the bad luck?
- ◆ How come I'm such a loser?
- ◆ Why can't someone give me a break?
- ◆ When will my life start to take off?
- ◆ Why do I always have such lousy relationships?

Such questions lead to the pain of helplessness and frustration and low self-esteem. Is there a question like this that you keep asking yourself over and over again, which tortures you endlessly and doesn't seem to have an answer? Think of such a question as a **wrong door** for you to go through.

My wrong doors

Make a list of any negative and critical questions that you ask yourself when you are in the low self-esteem loop. Reflect on this list and the feelings that you have when you question yourself in this way.

Now consider this: how many times do you need to ask yourself a self-defeating and unproductive question before you can stop and realise that this is a wrong door for you?

When you next find yourself looking low self-esteem in the eye, just stop and remember that *you can always change your responses*; you don't have to go down that well-worn path of negativity. Our habitual patterns have been learned and they can be unlearned. Get out of the self-blame game and stop punishing yourself. Let yourself off these self-defeating hooks and nurture your positive self-belief. You can do this: you only need to think you can!

Give yourself a break, and another one and another one. . .

53

SAY WHAT YOU MEAN

Clients often say that they never seem to be able to get what they want: life treats them badly and people treat them badly, so how can they feel good about themselves?

Well, we can only get what we want if we ask for what we want. This may seem obvious and yet we often don't ask for what we want because we don't always say what we mean. Have you ever had a conversation like this?

YOU: (wanting to go out to an Indian restaurant) 'Let's eat out tonight.'

PARTNER: 'OK.'

YOU: 'Where do you want to go?'

PARTNER: 'I don't care.'

YOU: 'Well let's decide on somewhere.'

PARTNER: 'I don't care, wherever you want.'

YOU: 'No, you decide.'

PARTNER: 'OK, let's go for a pizza.'

YOU: 'OK.' (As usual, I never get my way.)

Next time you don't get what you want, check that you asked for it clearly. Did you say what you meant or did you hold back for some reason? Start saying exactly what you mean and asking for what you want. Your feelings of self-respect will increase, and you will have much more chance of getting what you want.

Say what you mean and mean what you say and your life will become much simpler.

54

SOFTEN YOUR FOCUS

This world is a wonderful place.

How do you respond to this statement?

We often let our lives become humdrum and ordinary. As the years pass we are inclined to live our lives more and more according to our habits. Perhaps you always go through the same ritual when you get up in the morning, and such a habit may be useful because it saves time. However, habitual responses in our thought, behaviour and emotional processes can limit our experiences and take the magic and spontaneity from our lives. Here is a technique to lift you out of your habitual behaviour into a state of alert and enhanced awareness.

EXERCISE

Softening your focus

1 Next time you are walking down the street stare at the pavement or look ahead and

become aware of the focus of your vision. How far are you looking?

2   Now stop and expand your awareness. Rather than focus on one thing, expand your visual awareness. You will feel your focus 'softening' as you do this.

3   Become conscious of all those things in the corners of your vision; experience the colours and shapes of everything in your newly softened and enlarged focus.

4   Practise for a while and soon you will automatically begin to experience your environment in new ways. Extend and soften your focus in a social situation; you will be surprised at the additional information you will pick up about other people.

Look for more and you will experience more! Keep practising.

55

FEEL AMAZING, LOOK AMAZING

When did you last feel at your most beautiful?

Yes, it might have been that time when your hair looked great and your designer outfit was just right for the occasion; looking good can certainly give us a great boost of confidence and well-being. But let's not forget the times when you felt fabulous *even though* it was a bad hair day. When you remember these occasions you remind yourself of something that is vitally important: **you are only ever as attractive as you feel inside**.

My greatest feeling fabulous moments include the three times when I had just given birth, certainly very low in the glamour stakes but so high on excitement and love. Oh, and I can come away from the gym with the buzz of those feel-good endorphins rushing around my body; feeling great even though I'm hot and sweaty and my hair is sticking up.

The truth is that we always want to *feel* our best, and whilst this might also include looking good, *it doesn't depend on it*. If you are glowing with health and vitality then you feel amazing and look amazing because your aura will be charged with positive energy and you will look and feel full of life.

When you feel good you will look good because your energy will be buzzing.

– 56 –
CELEBRATE YOUR ORIGINALITY

To develop our self-esteem we need constant support and nurture; we need to recognise our intrinsic and unique worthiness.

EXERCISE

Tips on celebrating your uniqueness

Praise yourself for each success, however small it might seem to be. This will ensure that you appreciate *all* your achievements and stop the tendency to move the goalposts whenever you reach a goal.

Enjoy the unique qualities of others. However hard we try, there will always be someone who can improve on our performance. Learn from the achievements of others and add what you have learned to your own experience.

Enhance your originality. Whenever you feel the need to 'fit in' look carefully at what you feel are your differences. Stop trying to conform and accept and embellish your differences: these are what make you a unique and original person.

Ask yourself, 'Do I really want to do this?' Whenever you find yourself in a situation which is uncomfortable. Maybe you are facing a challenge that you need to deal with in order to grow. But possibly you are trying to do something that you feel you 'should' do, and it doesn't feel right. Check your deepest feelings: are you trying to please someone else at the expense of yourself?

Do something different. Self-esteem requires self-respect and it is hard to respect ourselves if we are stuck in a rut and afraid to try something new. So, give your dreams a chance!

Love your originality and enjoy your differences.

57

FEEL THE LOVE INSIDE YOU

Find a quiet, comfortable place and relax. Close your eyes and steady your breathing as you prepare yourself to let go of all the tension in your body and in your mind.

Start with your feet and taking one at a time consciously let go of any stress and pressure; relax your feet. And now relax your legs and then your abdomen and onwards up through your body, paying special attention to your back, neck, head and shoulder areas. When your whole body feels relaxed allow yourself time to enjoy this feeling of lightness.

Now relax your mind by ignoring the flow of continual thoughts. Each time you find yourself thinking just let the thought go and concentrate on your breathing. After a short while you will feel calmer.

Imagine your heart, see its perfect shape and know that it is full of love for you and the rest of the universe. Surround your heart with a beautiful pink light; this is the

light of your love. Feel this pink light surrounding you and encasing you in pure
love; yes, love is inside you.

Imagine sending your loving light out
into the world. Who do you know who
could do with some love right now?
Become aware of your feelings as you
broadcast love to others. The more love
you transmit the more love you feel.

Touch the love inside you, it is
always there just waiting for
you to feel it.

58

COME CLEAN WITH YOUR WANT LIST

If your intimate relationship is not all that you would wish it to be (the man in your life just isn't coming up with the goods), something has to crack and that doesn't have to be you. If you are fed up with living with an ostrich (with his head in the sand or the newspaper) it's time to come clean with your 'want' list.

You can't get what you want unless you can communicate your needs clearly and this might mean taking a new assertive but tactful approach.

Write a list of all the things that you want from your relationship. For example: *I want more emotional support, I want you to help around the house, I want to go out with you once a week* ... You might be surprised by what you come up with.

Women are not trained to put their needs first (we are always so busy looking after someone else). This time, put yourself first and stand up for what you want, but do this diplomatically. Don't read out your list in anger (this will never bring the changes you want).

Take one item at a time and communicate each of your needs in a way that is effective. Rather than criticising (you never take me out anywhere), use a supportive approach (I love going out with you, where shall we go this week?).

Communicate your needs in a creative way and you are more likely to get what you want.

59

ENJOY THE MUSIC OF THE SPHERES

We are busy people living in a busy world. Sometimes the demands of life can feel relentless as we rush around the universe doing this and doing that. When you feel caught on the treadmill of life ... STOP and try this simple and wonderful meditation technique.

EXERCISE

Climbing the ladder of sound

Get into a comfortable position where your head, neck and chest are in a straight line. You can lie down (as long as you don't fall asleep).

Now tune in to any inner sound that you can find in your head. Home in on that sound until it is the main sound that you can hear. Let all other sounds and thoughts pass by.

As you let this sound fill your consciousness you will ultimately merge with it so that you no longer hear it. At this point you will start to hear another sound. Now tune into this sound and repeat the process.

There are seven sounds, but it doesn't matter how many you think you hear because we all discriminate between sounds in a different way. The various descriptions of these sounds include: the song of the nightingale; the sound of cymbals; the ocean in a conch shell; the buzzing of bees; drumming and the sound of crowds in a large gathering place (such as a railway station). Listen for as long as you feel comfortable.

Don't bother to try to define the sounds, just relax and enjoy what is called the 'music of the spheres'.

60

TAKE A HOLIDAY

Your life is busy and it seems that everyone is making demands, so when can you get some time to yourself? Do you ever feel like this? Perhaps you need to look at your time management, but in the short term here's a quick little relaxer.

VISUALISATION:

Going on holiday

When you *do* have a few minutes to spare find a quiet place and sit down and relax. Close your eyes and become aware of your breathing. When your mind and body are feeling deeply relaxed, just imagine a tranquil and beautiful scene.

Choose an outdoor setting: by the beach, in the mountains, in a garden, wherever you like. Fill the scene with colour and detail, create your own wonderful holiday brochure photograph. Absorb the details of this place, see the sights, smell the fragrances, hear the birdsong, the running water, the waves crashing against the rocks. When you have created your ideal spot slowly return into the room and open your eyes.

Now you can go on holiday whenever you like. It only takes a second to get there, there's no packing and it's absolutely free. You can go at any time in any situation. When the going gets rough close your eyes for a few seconds, visualise your dream place and just be there! You really can get away from it all and come back feeling refreshed, without anyone knowing that you even left.

Perfect this technique. It really is fantastic.

– 61 –

CHANGE YOURSELF

You can make changes in a relationship only when you are ready to alter the messages that you are sending to the other person. Each time you focus on the other person you are looking in the wrong direction. Try this exercise that will prove this to be true.

EXERCISE

Seeking to change a relationship

- Think of a time when you tried to change someone.

- Describe the behaviour that you wanted to change.

- How did you try to change this behaviour?

- What was the outcome?

- Describe the sort of relationship that you have with this person now.

- Did your attempts to change this person have any effect on your relationship? If so, what happened?

- Have you ever recognised a repeating pattern of behaviour in your relationships?

- Have you ever stayed in an unhappy relationship?

- If so, why did you stay?

- How did you feel about the other person involved?

- Are you still in this relationship?

- How do you feel about yourself?

Think about your answers and look to see where your own feelings about yourself have been reflected back by someone else. If you value and respect yourself then you will only have relationships with people who appreciate you. Why would you spend time with someone who didn't?

Change yourself and your relationships will change.

62

STOP ARGUING

Are you stuck in a relationship crisis yet again? Has he let you down; been an idiot; behaved badly? Has she had another emotional outburst and left you feeling exhausted and confused? Is this relationship worth all the hassle? If your intimate relationship is an emotional roller-coaster ride then maybe it's time to reassess the situation.

When you find yourself locked in argument with your partner (yet again) you need to check out the following exercise.

EXERCISE

Why are you arguing?

1 Do you feel as if you are going over and over the same old issue that has come up before? In other words do you recognise a pattern here?

2 Are you feeling victimised, criticised or abused in some way? Is your partner really

treating you badly or are you feeling super-sensitive and vulnerable? Again, have you had this feeling before? Is there a pattern in your reaction?

3   Are you blaming each other rather than looking for a solution to your disagreements? If so, you are in a negative cycle which only leads to more anger and resentment.

4   Do you like the ups and downs of a yo-yo relationship (making up is just so sweet)?

Do you want to make this relationship work? Is it worth the effort? If it is, then talk to your partner about your feelings. Work together to overcome your difficulties. And if your relationship is going nowhere recognise this and leave!

☆ ☆ ☆

Understand why you are arguing and resolve your relationship crisis.

63

CREATE PEACE OF MIND

Being at peace does not mean losing touch with reality and escaping into a dream world, it means exactly the opposite. As soon as our mind stops whirling we are able to tap into a great source of energy. When our minds are peaceful we feel harmonious and balanced, we are able to communicate well and make effective decisions, we feel relaxed and in control and life is a joy. Try the following two exercises to help you to create peace of mind.

EXERCISE 1:

Memorise peacefulness

The next time you see a beautiful natural scene, close your eyes and commit the view to memory. Make a collection of peaceful scenes and memories and replay them whenever you feel the need. When we tap into visions of serenity and harmony we re-experience the positive feelings. Let the pictures cross your mind; they act like a healing balm.

Act instead of reacting

Peace comes when we take assertive charge of our lives instead of behaving like a passive victim. When a problem comes along don't waste your energy worrying, getting upset and *re-acting*. Stop and face the problem, decide the best way to tackle it and then *act*. When we are dealing courageously with our lives we gain self-respect and peace of mind.

Try this two-fold approach. The visualisation will work at the spiritual level and the assertive technique works at a behavioural level. Peace of mind allows us to realise our full creative and amazing potential.

Realise your own potential.

– 64 –

START TODAY TO MAKE
YOUR DREAMS COME TRUE

Have you ever heard people saying things like: *I've always wanted to go there, do that, have one of those, visit that place, start that business, begin that hobby*? Why didn't they ever do these things? When we know what we would love to do, we can start taking steps towards our dreams. Try the following exercise to discover your goals.

E X E R C I S E

Ten things I want to do in my life

I want:

To ....

To ....

To ....

To ....

To ....

To ....

To   ....
To   ....
To   ....
To   ....

Are you taking steps towards doing any of these things? If not, then why not? Focus on the steps you need to take to achieve your goals. Don't be a person who complains that they never got what they wanted out of life or you will always be disappointed and have low self-respect. Reach for the stars, take a risk, be courageous and ACT!

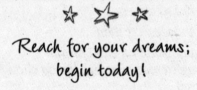

Reach for your dreams;
begin today!

STOP COMPARISON SHOPPING

Just watch those TV adverts! If only we use 'such and such' product we too will look as elegant/be as confident/sound as intelligent/be as thin/look as young/be as fit ... as whom?

When we are feeling low we often compare ourselves unfavourably with others. We go 'comparison shopping' where we 'buy into' the concept of a comparative scale of self-worth:

I'm not as clever as ...

But I'm cleverer than ...

I'm not beautiful enough/thin enough/creative enough/good enough to do that.

Do you ever compare yourself with others? How do we know if we are clever/ confident / happy / worthy / doing well / doing badly ... etc?

No one else can be inside you. No one

else can experience your self-satisfaction (or lack of it). Only you know what it feels like to be you. Stop comparison shopping, it will never do you any good because it will always keep you feeling negative and low in self-esteem. Every time you compare yourself with someone else become aware of what you are doing and stop it!

Say instead: *I am good enough.*

If we pursue the lifestyle dream of 'having it all' we will spend our whole lives trying to 'fit it' and be someone we are not. Be yourself, accept yourself, appreciate yourself!

You are a special and unique person and you are irreplaceable.

– 66 –

TAKE CONTROL OF YOUR RELATIONSHIPS

With your relationships reflecting back to you your deepest beliefs about yourself you have the perfect training course right on your doorstep. So how can you make the most of this reality workshop?

EXERCISE

Your reality workshop

Instead of looking outside yourself and blaming others for what is lacking in your relationships you can stop and answer these two important questions:

1. What is this relationship showing me about myself?

2. How can I use this insight to improve the relationships that I attract?

Think about any relationship that you are struggling with right now, and ask yourself these two questions and then:

- Dig deep and look for any repeating thought, behaviour or emotional patterns that you are experiencing.

- Ask yourself if you have experienced these patterns before with this person.

- Have you ever acted out these patterns with another person?

- What does this relationship reveal to you about yourself?

- Are there any ways that you could change your patterns so that they become more positive and useful?

If you are in a poor relationship and you keep on behaving and reacting in the same ways then the relationship will stay the same. Change yourself and the relationship will change or it will end.

You are in control.

67

HAVE A POWERFUL
SELF-IMAGE

Our self-belief and our view of the world depend largely on what we learned to believe as a child. If you were given love and support and were validated when you were tiny you are more likely to have a good strong self-image than someone who was criticised and invalidated.

Similarly you were 'taught' your beliefs about the world (*it's a benevolent universe/life's a bitch/people are basically good/everyone's out to get you ...*). Take your pick. What sort of pictures of the world were you brought up with?

Change any negative self-images; they will always stand in the way of your spiritual development. The way to do this is very simple. Just pinpoint your negative self-beliefs, throw them out and replace them with positive self-beliefs.

Example:

MY NEGATIVE SELF-BELIEFS	REPLACEMENTS
I'm no good at …	*I'm getting better at …*
I'm useless	*I'm a creative person*
I can't do that	*I'll do the best I can*
Trust me to make a mess of it	*I can make a good job of this*

Whenever negativity strikes, strike back with your new positive affirmations. What could be easier? Don't get wrapped up in an intellectual or emotional game with yourself. Negative beliefs serve no purpose, you were taught to believe they were true and now you believe them. That's all there is to it. Teach yourself something more useful.

Change a headful of negativity into a headful of positivity.

68

GIVE YOUR BACK A REST

So many people suffer with backache. Poor posture, too much sitting and too little exercise can aggravate the problem. If you measure yourself when you get up and then measure yourself again at the end of your busy day you will have shrunk as much as an inch. Gravity puts pressure on the discs between your vertebrae, muscles become shorter and joints become jammed together. No wonder we feel de-energised! Try to find a few minutes each day to allow your spine to lengthen, to loosen up your back muscles and to recharge your batteries.

Taking a moment's rest

Lie down on your back, upper arms resting on the floor and hands resting on your abdomen.

Support your head with a small cushion so that your head is in line with the rest of your body.

Pull up your legs, knees pointing to the ceiling. Keep your knees apart (about shoulder width) and your feet flat on the floor. Feel how this brings your lower back closer to the floor.

Rest like this for just a few minutes every day and feel the difference in your energy levels.

Give your back a break and
take a few restful moments out
of your busy day; the rewards
will be worth it!

– 69 –

CREATE SUCCESS FOR YOURSELF

Your imagination is very powerful; it can create whatever it chooses. Decide to create success for yourself. Say the following affirmation:

I deserve success

EXERCISE

Visualise your success

Find a comfortable place, close your eyes and relax. Follow your breathing until you feel deeply relaxed and then see your success in action. Picture the scene that you would like to create. See yourself being successful ... you look so confident and relaxed. Feel what it is like to be a winner. See people treating you with the respect that you deserve. Make the vision as real as you can: see and hear the whole thing in glorious Technicolor, create the sound effects and feel the reality of your success. When you are ready, let your thoughts return and open your eyes.

If you have negative thoughts when you are visualising, just let them go. This technique is very powerful and in fact is one that we use all the time. We often use our imagination in a negative way to support negative beliefs about ourselves. For example, we can use a negative affirmation (a belief that 'I can't do that') and support it with a negative visualisation (when, in our imagination, we see ourselves failing). So you see you are using these techniques all the time. Why not use them to create a positive outcome?

Use positive affirmations and visualisations to create the success you deserve.

70

BE BRAVE AND BOLD

What is worrying you? What are you afraid of? What is standing in your way? Our fears are usually groundless and our biggest fear is of fear itself: we are afraid of being afraid! The trick is to feel the fear and do it anyway: be big, brave and bold and you will discover hidden strengths and abilities. The greatest antidote to fear is boldness so tackle your obstacles in fighting spirit.

EXERCISE

Be bold

Reflect on any situation in your life where fear is standing in your way. You might be afraid to take a risk or to change your behaviour or even just to stand up for yourself. Now answer the following questions.

1 What exactly do you fear? Be as specific as possible here.

2. How would you need to change your thoughts so that you could THINK BOLDLY about this situation?

3. What would you need to believe about yourself to become assertive and go-getting?

4. How would you need to change your behaviour so that you could ACT BOLDLY?

5. What is the very first step that you need to take?

6. Take it now!

Boldness releases powerful forces into the universe. Whenever we act boldly and give it all we've got, our bodies go into a state of emergency and unlock many of the underused powers that we all possess, such as: stamina, endurance, strength, flexibility, commitment and focus.

Face your fear.
Think boldly. Act boldly.
Feel amazing.

71

ATTRACT AMAZING RELATIONSHIPS

It's important to remember that you attract the type of relationship that you think you most deserve. If you act like a victim you will attract a bully (your energies will be magnetic to each other).

We are highly influenced by our parents' relationship both with us and with each other. For example, if your parents were over-demanding of you when you were small you might still be creating relationships with people who ask too much of you; if your parents were emotionally close and supportive you are more likely to re-create such a relationship for yourself.

Our intimate relationships are always a reflection of our inner needs and expectations. If our parents had damaging relationship patterns then we might still be trying to work them out in our own relationships. There is nothing unusual about this; in fact we are all a product of our patterns.

The trick is to recognise where we are stuck and how we can change. And the key to change in relationships is the knowledge that it all begins with you.

You can never change anyone else; you can only change yourself. As you learn to love and respect yourself you will attract loving and respectful relationships.

All your relationships are a reflection of the one that you have with yourself.

72

MAKE THE MOST OF YOUR SELF

Modern make-up techniques and fabulous new products make it possible for us to minimise and maximise whatever we wish in our appearance. If you think your eyes are too close together, your lips too thin, your skin too blotchy ...

You only have to take yourself off for a professional makeover (at the make-up counter in a good department store) to learn the tricks to disguise the bits that you want to hide and to make the most of your assets. Take the time to find out how you can look your best and which products suit you.

And the same with your hair. Spend money on a really good stylist and get a great cut. Watch the blow-drying technique so that you can do it at home and ask advice on hair products that will be best for you.

If you want to know what suits you

there are plenty of experts around. Image specialists and colour consultants can open up new possibilities for you; try them if you need a change.

Develop a look and a style that suit you. Don't buy clothes just because they are fashionable or because they look good on someone else. Cultivate you own individual image, and you will become known for your originality and sense of personal flair.

Have fun with new products and fashion, and try re-inventing yourself. Your look is any look that you love; so get adventurous whenever you feel like a change.

Create a look that makes you feel great, and when you tire of it just change it.

73

BECOME AN OPTIMIST

Is your cup half full or half empty? Is your cake half eaten or have you still got half left? In other words, would you say that you are an optimist or a pessimist? Most of us are a bit of both. We can wake up feeling good, sing in the shower, smile at the world ... and the world will smile back; on such a day we can cope with whatever life throws at us. When things are not so good it's harder to keep upbeat and easy to fall into a cycle of depression.

Take an ordinary day when nothing is particularly terrible or wonderful. You wake up and ... how do you greet this day? Is this a perfect day or just twenty-four hours of hassle? Is your life a precious gift or are you just struggling to survive? Believe it or not you can *choose* the quality of your experiences: it's not *what* happens to you that counts but rather how you deal with what happens to you.

This Law of Attraction states that *we create whatever we think about.* We live within an electromagnetic field and each thought we have charges the energy field with vibrations. Like attracts like and this is the reason why grumpy people really *are* always having such a bad time (negative thought patterns attract all forms of negativity) and why upbeat people attract the good vibrations (positive thought patterns attract all forms of positivity).

Positive thinking is a powerful tool that will attract the very best into your life.

74

TOUCH YOUR SOUL

When we look at our lives we are often tempted to think that if only *this* would happen or I could meet *that* sort of person or if something would change, *then* I could be content.

A happy family, a meaningful career, enough money, good health, all these things are important and enhance the quality of our lives but they are not enough to create complete fulfilment. What price is peace? Where can we find it?

Peace, contentment, fulfilment and harmony are felt by the spiritual part of our being. Soul food cannot be bought at the supermarket. If the words 'spiritual' and 'soul' mean very little to you, think about a time when you felt 'touched' by something greater than yourself, when the world became a shining place for a moment. Let's touch that shining essence again.

Finding the soul's breath

1 Sit in a comfortable and quiet place. Close your eyes and relax.

2 Put your right hand over your heart and say to yourself, 'I breathe the soul's breath.'

3 Exhale and wait until your breath comes in by itself. Pause briefly as your breath reaches its fullness and then let it go.

4 Wait until your breath naturally comes to fill the space; as you do this you will feel that the breath is coming to you rather than that you are doing something.

When your breath is coming to you in this way you are consciously breathing the soul's breath.

Do this exercise and you will feel divine.

75

DE-STRESS YOURSELF

This might be hard to believe, but the truth is that nothing is actually stressful in itself. *Stress lies in the eye of the beholder.* In other words, if you perceive a person, situation or event as threatening, then your mind, body, spirit and emotions will register stress.

EXERCISE

Reframing your situation

Think of a personal situation that is a problem for you right now. It could be to do with a relationship, work, family or confidence. Choose something that is causing you worry and tension.

1 Find a quiet place, relax, close your eyes and visualise the problem in glorious Technicolor. See it as vividly as you can. Hear the sounds and really feel all your emotions connected with this problem.

2 Now, take the person/event/situation and drain all the colour and vibrancy, sound and

emotion out of your scenario.

3 Imagine the image getting smaller and smaller, shrinking until it has totally disappeared.

4 Now create a big, bold and colourful picture of you dealing brilliantly with the situation. See yourself looking confident, finding a resolution to the problem and see, feel and hear your success.

Use this technique to change any negative aspects of your life.

See the image.

Drain the colour.

Shrink the picture.

See and feel a bright new positive image.

Reframe your negative pictures and take the stress out of your life.

76

TEACH YOUR CHILDREN WELL

Only our negative beliefs stand between us and our self-esteem, and we learned most of these beliefs in our childhood.

We know so much today about the power of positive thinking and the results of negative criticism. For those of us who are parents this knowledge is invaluable. Words are so powerful and they can be used to encourage and support or to belittle and tease. We know that babies and tiny children believe what we teach them to believe. If they are told that they are stupid, useless, no good, worthless, lazy, etc., they will believe these things to be true about themselves and they will grow up with little confidence and low self-esteem, which inevitably leads to poor behaviour patterns.

With the knowledge and awareness that we now possess, we can encourage and empower our children by supporting them in a positive way. This does not mean that we tell them that everything they do is marvellous – far from it.

We can:

◆ Admire our children and tell them how much we love them and how special they are.

◆ Encourage them to discuss their feelings.

◆ Show them ways to do things without belittling their own attempts.

Each time you encourage a person to increase their self-esteem your own sense of value increases. Empower your children and help to secure a generation of young people who are high in self-esteem.

Encourage and empower your children and they will know how to respect themselves and others.

77

ACCEPT A COMPLIMENT

I take a lot of trouble to look nice for a party.

You: *'Oh you look lovely in that dress, is it new?'*

Me: *'What, this old thing? I've had it ages – I bought it in a sale.'*

I spend a lot of time and effort on writing a report.

You: *'This is a brilliant piece of work, you have obviously put a lot of time and effort into it.*

Me: *'Oh, it was nothing.'*

I cook a special meal.

You: *'This food is delicious. You really are a good cook.'*

Me: *'No, I'm not really, I just threw a few things together.'*

Why do we find it so hard to accept a compliment gracefully? How do you feel when someone openly admires you? Do you ever make throwaway comments that spoil the effect of a compliment because you are feeling embarrassed? We are all inclined to do this, and the result is that we belittle the compliment and devalue the opinion of the person giving it. How do you feel if you compliment someone and they don't accept it? Would you bother to do it again?

Whenever someone congratulates, encourages and supports you they are showing you respect and admiration. If you 'throw away' their compliment you are only showing your lack of self-esteem.

Learn to accept a compliment. The next time someone says something nice about you just say 'thank you'.

Accept a compliment and you will feel wonderful and so will the person giving it.

78

LIVE IN HARMONY

Although we moan and complain about people, we know, deep down, that we feel at our most positive and optimistic about life when we are communicating and working successfully with others. Human beings are here to learn to live and to work together and whenever we achieve this in some way, we feel really great (we reach a team target at work for example, or perhaps our relations come together to celebrate a family event). So how can we overcome potential social discord and tricky group encounters? How can we learn to tolerate each other's differences?

Seven ways to live in harmony

1 **Always try to bring out the best in people.** Remember that others are as shy as you are and they don't always feel confident enough to show their best side.

2 **But don't be a victim!** Always expect

others to treat you well. If you carry a sense of unworthiness about with you it is likely to draw potential bullies and victimisers into your arena.

3 **Respect yourself** and your ideas and others will mirror your feelings.

4 **Be tolerant** of the shortcomings of others.

5 **Be a good listener** and new doors will open for you; try this today!

6 **Say what you mean.** Be straightforward, people appreciate it if they know where they stand with you.

7 **Always remember that people come first.** The most important element of any encounter is always the personal one: people matter most.

Strive for harmony and overcome discord: people matter.

79

LOVE THIS MOMENT

When you can bring your full attention to the present moment you will feel happy. All your worries and anxieties are about the future (what might or might not happen) or about the past (regrets, guilt, recriminations, lack of forgiveness ... etc).

Try out this theory. Think about your anxieties, all those things that are stopping you from feeling happy right now and you will find that they have yet to happen or that they are already part of the past. Why do you burden yourself so unnecessarily? The only time we ever really have is NOW!

Sometimes when clients get over-involved in the past or worry about the future I ask them to stop and tell me where they are. Where is this place where that action happened? Where is this place that they are so worried they will reach? And the answer of course is **nowhere**! There is no past or future; the past has gone, the future is yet to come; only the present moment is real!

If you load the future with negative concerns then this is what you will draw into your life. The beliefs, thoughts and visualisations that you are having in the present are creating your future NOW! So be mindful of this moment, live it and love it and you will both feel happy *and* create a happy future.

The present is aptly named.
Appreciate the gift of this
moment.

80

RECOGNISE THE POWER OF POSITIVITY

Try this experiment with a friend.

Step 1 Stand facing each other and put your left hand on her right shoulder.

Step 2 Ask her to extend her left hand, palm down, elbow straight and wrist slightly higher than her shoulder. (It doesn't matter which side of the body you use as long as your hand rests on your partner's opposite shoulder.)

Step 3 Now ask her to think of something that makes her feel really good. (She should close her eyes and imagine this as clearly as possible.) When she's ready tell her that you are going to try to push down her extended hand and that she should resist this pressure (her eyes can be open or closed).

Step 4 Place your fingers on her arm just beyond her wrist (between wrist and elbow) and press down. Make a note of the power of her resistance.

Step 5 Now ask your friend to close her eyes and think of something very negative. When she's ready repeat the process, putting your right hand on her arm and pressing down. You will both be amazed when her arm goes straight down with no strength in it at all. Reverse roles and watch it happen again!

This incredibly simple experiment demonstrates how profoundly we are affected by positive and negative thoughts and feelings: we really can choose to create a positive or negative reality just by our attitude.

Make a positive choice and change your life.

81

TAKE A RAINBOW SHOWER

Whenever you need a lift, whether it is to energise yourself or to throw light on a problem, try taking a shower of light. You can do this at any time, in any place, and no one will be any the wiser.

Visualising a shower of light

Imagine that you are standing under a shower. See large drops of white light falling over you and enveloping you.

Feel the light as it embraces you.

See the white light turn into the colours of the rainbow and immerse yourself in the colours.

Choose any colour which you feel particularly drawn to (this is the colour that you need right now) and spend a few moments bathing in this coloured light. Feel and absorb this colour. Be aware of the properties of this colour entering your mind, body and spirit.

If another colour comes to mind, repeat

the process. Take all the colours that you need. When you are ready, mentally turn off the shower.

The rainbow shower of light is a spiritual cleansing of your whole being and you can do it anywhere, it only takes a moment.

Try putting your co-workers in a shower of light and notice the difference in your working day!

The rainbow shower is a
wonderful experience both to
have and to give.
Just try it.

82

BE A REBEL

Small people are so good at letting us know how they feel, aren't they? They are not averse to a good shout and stamp when necessary. Well, I'm not suggesting that you have a tantrum, but you could try some natural ways to reduce stress and anxiety. Get in touch with your childish playfulness and rebelliousness and enjoy the following exercise, which has a really de-stressing and calming influence.

EXERCISE

The 'you can't make me' swing

Stand with your feet apart (about the width of your shoulders). Swing your body, neck and head as one unit to the left and then to the right. Let your arms swing freely as your body turns from side to side, so that they wrap around you at your shoulders. Make sure that your head follows your body as you swing.

As your body swings from left to right and back, shout, 'You can't make me!' as loud as possible.

Enjoy yourself. Keep shouting. Try 'I don't care' or 'No I won't'.

Letting go of anger and pent-up frustration in this way is good for self-respect and also introduces a very important humorous touch. When we are low in self-esteem we are inclined to take ourselves far too seriously.

Swing, shout and laugh and
bring everything back into
perspective.

83

DON'T GIVE YOUR POWER AWAY

Guilt and blame are always hanging around, ready to be used whenever things aren't looking so clear. *'He left me, what did I do wrong?' 'The children are out of control, I must be a bad parent.'* Whether we blame someone else or ourselves, we remain a victim. Self-empowerment comes when we can step out of *all* blame and guilt and view our circumstances with a degree of objectivity.

EXERCISE

Are you giving your power away?

Sit quietly for a few moments. Close your eyes and imagine yourself full of vibrant and dynamic energy. Feel the power within you and then feel yourself sending this force out into the world.

Yes, you really are a powerhouse of amazing energy, but how are you using this resource? We can give away our power in many ways. The following list shows how we might be doing this.

- Recognising a problem and blaming someone else (now we have to wait for them to do something about it).

- Blaming ourselves (losing self-respect and confidence).

- Waiting for someone to change (we will quite possibly be waiting forever).

- Looking to the past with regret and blame.

- Looking to the future in fear.

- Waiting for *anything* to change (being passive and reactive).

Each time we try to find the solutions to our problems by looking outside ourselves for answers, we allow our energy to leak away.

Look inside for your answers;
you have all the power you
need.

84

FOLLOW YOUR STAR

You are the one and only you. Only you can make the contribution you came here to make. Your combination of special talents is unique and irreplaceable. You have come for a special purpose, to fulfil your life's work. Have you discovered your life's work?

You will know when you are not doing your life's work because you will feel dissatisfied, incomplete, low in self-esteem, low in energy and generally out of sorts. These feelings indicate that you have wandered from your path. The following visualisation is a powerful way to get back on course.

VISUALISATION
Attracting your life's work

Sit quietly, relax and close your eyes. Imagine that your life's work can be represented by a symbol. Visualise what that symbol would be; take the first thing that comes to mind.

Hold your symbol close to your body and feel its energy filling your whole being. Sense this energy entering every cell of your body.

You see a hill ahead of you. Carry your symbol to the top. The journey is easy and your symbol is light.

At the top of the hill you see an arched gateway. Stand under this archway and look behind you and see your past. Give thanks for all the experiences it has taken to reach where you are today.

Step through the gateway and release your symbol – this is your future.

Your symbol is spinning through the universe attracting to itself the ways and means for you to find your true purpose in life.

85

LET YOURSELF OFF THE HOOK

When I work with a group I sometimes stop whatever we are doing and ask them to think of three things that they don't like about themselves. This exercise only takes a few minutes – everyone can think of *at least* three things and they are never reluctant to tell the rest of the group.

Then I ask everyone to think of three things that they like about themselves. This is always so much more difficult and most people can't think of one thing let alone three, and no one really wants to tell everyone else anything nice about themselves. Why is this? Why is it so much easier for us to bring ourselves down than it is to lift ourselves up? Try this exercise yourself.

Things I like and don't like about myself

Three things I don't like about myself:

. . . .

Three things I like about myself:

. . . .

Did you find it hard to praise yourself? Was it easy to criticise yourself? Deep down we are all excessively self-critical; even the most confident people have a well-developed inner critic. Our inner critic is that part of us that is never ever satisfied with what we do. Recognise that you can never satisfy its overbearing demands and just move on.

Stop bringing yourself down, let yourself off the critical hook and concentrate on your achievements.

86

ATTRACT A POSITIVE LOVE RELATIONSHIP

You will only have great relationships when you are ready to take responsibility for yourself. Once you accept that the qualities of your thoughts and beliefs help to create the quality of your life then you are well on your way to going for and achieving whatever it is you want.

A positive approach keeps you motivated and enthusiastic and this energy always attracts fresh possibilities and new relationships; yes there really are many fish in the sea, you just have to get out there with your rod!

The negative view will create self-doubt and insecurity and an inability to take assertive action, so if a likely love interest does swim by it might be just too scary to bait your line and reel him in.

Whether your thoughts and beliefs are positive or negative will obviously have a great impact on the type of people you attract and the sort of relationship choices you make. An optimistic outlook always brings a feeling of hopefulness and confidence to any situation and this automatically opens the door to new prospects in life (and love). It's so simple: negativity attracts negativity and positivity attracts positivity. So radiate whatever it is you want to attract. When you demonstrate enthusiasm and motivation you uplift the energy of those around you and draw similarly positive people into your orbit.

The type of relationships you attract depends entirely upon the type of energy you project.

87

TAKE A NATURAL BREAK

The best things in life are free!

Go outside and notice the natural world. Even if you are in the middle of a city you can find a park, a tree, a bird, some blossom.

Take a few minutes away from your thoughts to appreciate the beauty of nature. Look at the perfection of a flower, of the passing clouds, the sunshine, the rain.

Be thankful for the beauty that surrounds you and value the miracle of your life.

Don't let your busyness take you over completely. Find time every day to connect with the natural rhythms of the universe. If you can do this regularly you will feel more grounded and in touch with your emotions and thoughts. Become more aware of the natural world and look for the wonder that constantly surrounds you. Give love and appreciation to life and you will find that it will be returned to you in so many ways.

Take a natural break whenever you can and remind yourself that you are a child of the universe. Feel your deep connection with nature and always remember that you are a creature of the earth and that this is where your roots lie.

Slow down, get into the natural rhythms and just feel the difference this makes!

88

MAKE A POSITIVE IMPRESSION

Cast your mind back to the last time you were faced with a group of strangers, perhaps at a party, a work-training event or a job interview.

Faced with the unknown our adrenaline starts rushing and our behaviour can become erratic. The person who can survive the pressure is the one who has high self-esteem and feels free to be herself.

The truth is that everyone feels intimidated sometimes in their lives but the person who survives such feelings is the one who has an open mind and can see the lighter side of life: the pessimist will look for problems and find them and the optimist will act spontaneously and creatively. We all know which of these two types we would want on our team. Look at the following checklist. What are your own positive and negative traits?

Personality checklist

1 Fear of rejection (negative)

2 Good sense of humour; can laugh at self (positive)

3 Worried about not being liked (negative)

4 Genuinely likes people and shows interest in them (positive)

5 Has to have the last word, must be right (negative)

6 Can say sorry when necessary (positive)

7 Self-centred (negative)

8 Good listener (positive)

9 Low self-esteem (negative)

10 Doesn't take things personally (positive)

To eliminate the negative just accentuate the positive and you will make a fabulous impression.

89

IMPROVE YOUR SEX LIFE

Physical attraction is always so strong at the beginning of a relationship. The tantalising nature of the mating game, attracting and seducing, leaves the hormones in a perpetual state of excitement and the beloved is an amazingly erotic hero/heroine who can do no wrong. No wonder the sex is good! And then, if the fairytale comes true and we become a 'stable relationship', everything changes.

Increasing commitment and responsibility to each other bring peace and security and those early days of thrilling sexual excitement come to an end. Things like jobs, children and mortgages inevitably affect our sex lives. But it is possible to keep your sex life buzzing in a long-term (children/mortgage/jobs/shopping/drain-cleaning/putting out the rubbish) relationship.

Concentrate on sex

Focus your attention on your sex life. If it's losing its appeal, talk about it to each other.

Keep talking about sex with each other (whenever possible). We can be sexual all day; we don't have to wait until we get into bed at night!

Put the romance back into your relationship. What turned you on in the first place? Recreate that atmosphere once again.

Laugh together. When we share humour we bring greater intimacy to our relationship.

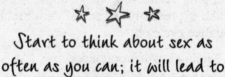

Start to think about sex as often as you can; it will lead to great things!

90

SMILE AND THE WORLD SMILES WITH YOU

When we are low in confidence our energy becomes depressed and we find it hard to communicate with other people and to appreciate anything about our lives. Our energy turns inward because we are all tied up with feeling bad about ourselves, and it can feel impossible to rise up out of this negativity.

Sometimes we can break this cycle by changing something very simple – like a facial expression. A smile can break a negative cycle of:

◆ Feeling low in confidence

◆ Looking dejected and feeling unable to communicate with others

◆ Others stopping communicating with us

◆ Enhanced feelings of low self-confidence (I am so worthless that people don't bother with me any more).

Look into the mirror and smile. Really smile with all of your face – eyes as well as mouth. Look closely; can you see how it lights up your face and changes the energy that you radiate? Take your smile for a walk, practise it in the presence of others and watch how it changes the way that people respond to you.

Also notice how you feel so much better when you are smiling and laughing; they both give amazing health benefits as well as lifting our mood and making us feel great. Laughing is wonderful exercise: it deepens our breathing and improves our circulation, and smiles and laughter stimulate the production of our natural feel-good chemicals.

Just smile, you will feel great and so will everyone around you.

91

JUST DO IT

What is it that you would most love to do but are afraid to do because of the consequences? The following exercise will help you to judge how realistic your fears actually are.

EXERCISE

As good and as bad as it can be

1 Name three things that you would love to do but that you are afraid to try.

2 Ask yourself what would be the best and worst possible outcomes of doing each of these three things.

BEST POSSIBLE OUTCOME	WORST POSSIBLE OUTCOME
(i)	
....	
(ii)	
....	
(iii)	
....	

3 Ask yourself: 'What are my fears and anxieties?' and write them down.

4 Ask yourself, 'How realistic are these fears and anxieties?'

Rate your score for realism on a scale of 1–10, where
1 = TOTALLY UNREALISTIC
10 = TOTALLY REALISTIC

How realistic are your fears? If we long to do something and don't do it, that longing can last a lifetime. Usually our fears are irrational and groundless and our longing by far outweighs the reality of the fear.

Go ahead — just do it!
You will feel fantastic.

92

STOP FOR A BREATHER

If you stopped trying to be the best juggler in town, what do you think might happen? Will the sky fall in if you: don't get everything on the shopping list; make a quick snack for dinner; can't clear your in-tray by going-home time; forget to clean the floor; don't pick up your dry cleaning; don't have time to do the washing?

Ah, but there's so much to do! Yes, I agree, but surely it's time to take a stand when our lives become nothing more than a succession of repeated chores: there will *always* be more to do whilst we draw breath.

On a day when you are over-doing it, you will recognise your own symptoms; stop before they turn into a headache or anything equally unpleasant. Let the signs be a warning to you and take immediate action (or, rather, inaction).

Take a few moments to stand and stare (the world won't stop just because you have). Yes, you can easily find the time. When you incorporate 'being' time into your 'doing' time you will find that everything flows much more smoothly.

Try it now. Soften your gaze, let go of your thoughts, and allow yourself to drift off for a few seconds. It doesn't take long to create a more balanced awareness, which will then help you to put everything back into perspective.

Include some 'standing and staring' time in your busy schedule and you will feel more relaxed and in control.

93

TRANSFORM NEGATIVE ENERGY

Being positive does not mean that you always have to look on the bright side of life and push anything negative under the carpet. Positive people look realistically at life and they are not afraid of their own or other people's negativity. So don't hide away from thoughts, feelings and behaviour that are unhelpful and unsupportive, but recognise negativity when it arises in yourself and others, and then deal with the energy so that it can work for you.

Of course this might mean making a decision not to spend time with someone who brings you down; a conscious choice not to be that person's victim would be a good way to convert a negative situation into a positive outcome.

Overcoming negativity

Name three personal challenges which have pushed you into a negative state but which you went on to overcome. Look at each one separately and ask yourself the following questions:

- Why did I go down?
- How long did I stay there?
- What change in attitude caused my energy to lift and me to face my challenge?
- How did I overcome my negativity?
- How do I feel now I look back at this situation?

Looking back at difficulties is a very positive act. Here you will discover so much about yourself, your resourcefulness, your inner strength and your capacity to always bounce back.

You can and will overcome anything.

94

BE ASSERTIVE

Winners and losers communicate differently and this is their defining feature. Victims wheedle, whine and complain and non-victims use assertive communication skills.

Start to become aware of how assertive or non-assertive you are in different situations. Try out some of the following approaches.

Six ways to be assertive

1 **Be prepared to take risks** (no need to take up a dangerous sport, just be ready to make changes).

2 **Try to be less judgemental**. Withhold criticism and look for positive things to praise; people really respond to this approach.

3 **Become a listener**. You will be amazed by the effect this has. Refrain from having your say and listen

actively. Everyone responds well to this treatment.

4 **Say what you mean** and mean what you say. Open and honest communication makes it easy for others to know where they stand with you.

5 **Be ready to say 'no'** when you have to. This little word is often hard to say. Practise! I promise you it gets easier and easier the more you say it.

6 **Accept criticism without flying off the handle** immediately. Maybe she's got a point? If not, then say what you feel, but rationally and not in the heat of anger (this carries much more authority).

These techniques help to open the lines of communication and will work to heal rifts and differences.

When you are assertive you are respecting yourself and others.

95

DON'T WITHHOLD YOUR APPRECIATION

A client told me that he had spent his whole life trying to make his father proud of him. He had followed the same profession and the same football team and even lived in the same street. Although this man was married with his own children he was always waiting for his father to acknowledge his achievements.

When his father became very ill he spent a lot of time at his bedside. One day, not long before his death, the old man said to his son: 'My boy, you have always been a marvellous son and I am so proud of you.' My client said that he broke down and burst into tears as he heard the words that he had been waiting for all his life.

Don't hold back on your appreciation for people. Give credit where it is due and enjoy the feeling this brings you. Don't withhold your love because you feel embarrassed. Life is short; don't wait until it is too late to tell others how much they mean to you.

EXERCISE

Show your appreciation

- Who do you appreciate in your life? Name these people.

- Have you told them how you feel?

- Tell them at the very next chance you get. (Don't expect them to know how you feel; they won't know unless you tell them.)

When we show our love and appreciation for others their self-esteem rises and so does ours!

Whenever you help other people to feel good about themselves you will also feel better about yourself.

96

HEAL YOUR LIFE

'To heal' literally means 'to make whole' and every time we have a problem, whether it's mental, spiritual, emotional or physical, we are being shown a place where we need to heal ourselves (make ourselves whole). However good our doctor, psychotherapist, counsellor, osteopath, reflexologist, aromatherapist ... etc., we need to remember that ultimately our healing is in our own hands. Only we can choose to create health and balance in our lives.

However ill you feel, whatever psychological problems you face, you can still be in control of your own healing. If you have a physical condition find out all you can about it – don't just expect the doctor to 'sort you out'. Take the prescribed medicine but also investigate alternative approaches. Look at your lifestyle and nutrition; do they support good health? How about your relationships – are they supportive or stressful? Do you love your work or is it winding you up? Look beyond a single symptom; look at the *whole* picture of your life.

Healing yourself

Love yourself	Express your needs
Forgive yourself	Take care of your body
Release all blame	Trust your intuition
Release all negativity	Develop your self-esteem

Do these things and you will start to feel better and better and better!

Take charge of your own healing and you will be back in control of your life.

97

LET GO OF SELF-LIMITATIONS

If you feel dissatisfied about anything in your life you have the power to change it. Remember that indomitable will and creative spirit that you brought with you at birth? You still have these strengths; you only need to find them. Look into your past for the clues that you need to change your future. And then let go of any limitations that you discover; there are no limits unless you believe there are!

Our caretakers (parents, teachers etc.), often with the best will in the world, may have helped us to create a set of artificially low false ceilings, which will always stop us reaching the heights. These self-limiting beliefs and ideas can be changed. Yes you *can* do that! Of course you are clever enough to ... No, it's not too late to have riding lessons; go to art school; play the violin; take that exam; change your career path ...

Visualising the real you

Sit quietly, close your eyes and relax. Now imagine
that you are full of creativity and positivity. Feel the
energy that this brings. See yourself being
successful and happy and fulfilled. How do you
look? What are you doing? Who are you doing it
with? Play with your imagination and create some
great scenarios. Feel the atmosphere in the scenes;
hear the noises; smell the smells; really be there.
See the real you in full flow, with all the support and
help you need.

*Know that you are already on
the way to making your
visualisations come true.*

98

FEEL THE ENERGY

Imagine that you are about to open the door to a room where a party is going on. You step inside and look around and what do you notice? Well, you see the people and the room but this is not all that you take in.

At a subtler level you are *sensing* the energies of everyone there, you can feel the energetic vibrations in the room. If there is a buzz in the air you might 'catch' the excitement and if the energy is low you will probably get a sinking feeling in your solar plexus and start looking for the nearest exit.

Other people's energy can have a direct effect on the way that we feel and you don't need to have clairvoyant powers to sense at this intuitive level. We are all picking up on the thoughts and feelings of others as we go about our daily business but we are often doing this unconsciously.

Think about that time when you were

feeling great and you met someone who was full of complaints and moans. What happened to your brilliant mood? Unless you are consciously aware of the energy that surrounds you it's possible to be dragged down into the pits of negativity without even realising how it happened. Start to tune into others and feel the energy that they are radiating.

Spend time with positive and upbeat people and you will 'catch' their energy.

99

FOLLOW YOUR INTUITIVE GUIDANCE

Can you remember a time when you acted upon your intuition and things turned out well? What about a time when you 'knew' that you should do something but you didn't follow your gut feeling and things went badly for you?

Now think about your life at the moment. What intuitive guidance have you received recently? This might involve small changes: get the car serviced; phone a friend; take some time out for yourself; read that book. Or it may be pointing to much larger issues: end that relationship; stop smoking; train for a new job. Have you acted on this guidance? If not, why not?

Sometimes we just don't want to do what our heart and soul are telling us to do. When we receive inner guidance to make big changes in our lives we would often rather not listen and just keep on with our usual routine. If your intuition is sending strong messages that you are dis-regarding, then dissatisfaction and unhappiness are close at hand.

Start to make a habit of listening to your inner voice. Whenever you are uncertain of a decision or unsure how to act, take a moment to hear what your intuition is telling you. Act on hunches, gut feelings, flashes of insight and feelings of 'know-ingness' and see where they take you. Trust your inner knowing and it will guide you towards amazing new experiences.

Your intuitive guidance is always leading you to realise your full potential.

– 100 –
GET FIT FOR LIFE

We all know that exercise is good for our physical and mental health and that it will improve the way we look. But a good keep-fit regime requires a commitment of time, energy and motivation and it's easy to believe that we haven't any of these to spare. Do you recognise any of the following excuses?

Eleven ineffective excuses to stop you exercising

1 I find exercise so boring.
2 I'm basically a lazy person.
3 I haven't got the time.
4 My head hurts, my arm aches, etc.
5 I'm not a sporty type; I'm too uncoordinated.
6 I've been exercising for three weeks and nothing is happening.

7 I'm too fat to wear Lycra.

8 I can't stick at anything so I know I'd just give up too soon.

9 I can't afford to join a gym.

10 I'm too tired to be bothered.

11 I'm afraid to go to a gym; I won't know what to do and I am embarrassed by my flab.

If you are using any of these excuses it's time to admit that none of them is valid. Keeping fit does not mean that you have to become a top athlete. Nor does it mean that you need a perfect Lycra-clad body before you can get on an exercise bike. You don't even have to go near a gym when a good brisk daily walk will work wonders. Face your negative attitudes here and recognise how they are limiting you.

There is a direct relationship between exercise and a positive mood.

101

RADIATE POSITIVITY

Get comfortable, relax your body and relax your mind. Close your eyes and follow your breathing, in and out, in and out, in and out ... and soon you will find that your busyness has slowed down and that you are much calmer and more alert.

EXERCISE

Radiate love and kindness

Now, imagine that love and kindness are pouring into your heart; feel how much you are loved and appreciated.

Make this feeling even stronger and bigger until your heart is overflowing with love and kindness. Stay with this feeling for a while.

You are so full of love and positive energy that you want to send it out into the world. Start by sending this energy to your loved ones; in your mind's eye see them looking positive and strong and happy.

Is there anyone else you can think of who could

do with some of this powerful energy? Send them some.

Notice that the more you radiate this loving energy, the more fabulous you feel.

When you open your eyes maintain this warm loving feeling. You take your loving energy wherever you go, just tap into it wherever you are: at work; on a train; picking up the kids from school; cooking; out to dinner ... Practise radiating positivity and you will feel and look fantastic. And just see how wonderfully others react!

When you radiate positivity the whole world responds to you.

102

GET OUT OF THE BOX

Our personalities are complex; we have many voices and conflicting thoughts and emotions. We believe what we have learned to believe about our world and ourselves and we often find that these beliefs can stop us moving forward.

If you are plagued with a pessimistic disposition then it might be good to know that you can change this mood. If you are stressed and overburdened it really is possible to step beyond this feeling and to regain control of your life.

Perhaps in the attempt to *have it all* you are finding yourself *having to do it all*, but it doesn't have to be like this for you. It really is possible to relax and take control of your life. Hard to imagine? Well, start now!

Open yourself to infinite possibilities; believe that you have a purpose on this planet; know that you attract whatever you focus upon the most; be ready to step out of the box and become your true self!

Our personal vision of who we are can keep us stuck in the same old habits and grooves. But comfort zones are only comfortable until we outgrow them and then we feel confined, trapped and *un*comfortable.

This process (of moving on) is a natural one; we change, progress and evolve throughout our lives, and the trick is to be able to move along with this natural flow. Whenever you become aware that you have outgrown your comfort zone, just get out of that box!

Stop restricting and limiting yourself, step forward into a new space.

103

JUST FACE THE MUSIC AND DANCE

Are you stumbling through life trying to cope with things that are 'happening' to you? Do you sometimes feel like a victim? Notice those people who seem to dance through life at their own tempo. Who do you know who is like this? These people are happy and successful and are living their lives at their own pace; they are refusing to be victimised and have made a positive decision to meet life 'head on'.

'Just face the music and dance' is such a wonderful phrase. It conjures up the image of risk-taking, decision-making, accepting challenges and making things happen in an entirely non-threatening way. Maybe you will have to learn to say 'no' more often; you may have to put up with some people not liking you any more; others might become envious of you, but always remember, *whose life is this anyway?*

Dancing through your problems

Bring to mind all the problems that you have.
Picture them in your mind's eye, see them crowding
together, jostling for your attention. Now imagine
yourself clearing a pathway between the crowds.
Push the problems to the side and create a shining
path that leads you to your future. Visualise
yourself dancing along your path, recognising your
problems as you skip past, but not letting them
stand in your way.

Don't let your problems drag you down, dance
lightly through your life.

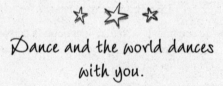

*Dance and the world dances
with you.*

104

ASSOCIATE WITH SUCCESSFUL PEOPLE

Do you admire your friends and colleagues, or are you associating with victims? Many people with low levels of confidence actually feel threatened by people who appear to be successful, choosing instead to spend time with those who are in an even worse situation than themselves.

EXERCISE

Check your motives

◆ Are you friends with that poor hapless person because you are really trying to help her to change her situation?

◆ Are you really helping her?

◆ Does she want to be helped?

◆ Are you enjoying feeling sorry for her?

◆ Do you feel more confident when you are with her because at least you are more together than she is?

If we choose to spend time with people who cannot handle success then we will become just like them.

Look for people who have gone before you and have made a success of whatever it is you are trying to achieve. Whichever area of your life you are trying to improve – your relationships, career, personal development, dress sense, parenting, etc. – check out those who have succeeded in your chosen area and learn from them.

Success attracts success, just as negativity attracts more negativity.

Mix with people you admire and you will feel inspired to create your own success.

105

CREATE YOUR OWN HEALTH FARM

Take a whole day for yourself and have a health farm extravaganza in the privacy of your own home. Planning is important so decide beforehand exactly how you will spend your day.

Planning your day

Buy any beauty items that you might need. Choose you favourite treatments: mud masks; aromatherapy oils for your bath; deep hair treatments; wax for legs (if you are brave) and anything else you would like to try but usually never have the time to.

Choose some beautiful relaxing music and some scented oils to burn so that you can create an atmosphere of peace and tranquillity. Candlelight encourages relaxation so buy some candles if you haven't any.

Choose a book or magazine to read. Get

something that you really enjoy rather than something that you think would be 'good' for you to read. Remember this is *your* day to spend as *you* wish.

Shop for some delicious nutritious food. Prepare it beforehand if you need to. Buy some pure fruit juice and bottled water to drink throughout the day (this helps to clear the mind and body of toxins).

Get together anything else that you think you will need to complete your day of pampering.

Start your day by switching off all phones, TVs and computers.

When you spend a day just pampering yourself you will feel refreshed and invigorated.

When we learn to appreciate ourselves we are learning to appreciate our lives.

106

GET CONFIDENT

Self-confidence opens the door to love, joy, happiness and fulfilment. But how can you lift your spirit and lighten your days when you find yourself in a negative spiral of low self-worth?

Confidence depends upon self-knowledge; the more you know about the way you tick the easier it will be to feel and act assertively. Stop dwelling on your weaknesses and start to concentrate on your strengths. When do you feel powerful and strong? Try the following quiz and find out exactly what does give you confidence.

QUICK QUIZ:
Ten things that give you confidence

1 I am at my best when ....

2 I feel really sexy when ....

3 I feel attractive when ....

4 My finest asset is ....

5 My personality strengths are ....

6 The most incredible thing I have ever done is . .

7 I feel empowered when . . . .

8 I love it when I . . . .

9 I am proud of myself for . . . .

10 The thing I like best about myself is . . . .

Look at your completed statements; what a fine description of a positive and motivated person. Confidence depends upon the way we see ourselves and if we keep bringing ourselves down that is where we will stay – down. So keep looking to your strengths and increase your self-awareness and you will find that the life you live will become more and more fascinating.

Think confident, feel confident,
act confident.

107

GO WITH THE FLOW

When we are going with the flow we feel inspired and carry an extra sense of purpose and clarity; there is a feeling of being in the right place at the right time, doing what we are supposed to do.

EXERCISE

Getting in the flow

Think of a time when you felt like this. Perhaps you were in a great relationship or you had started a new and exciting project.

Describe the situation. Remember your feelings of excitement and enthusiasm; a wonderful energetic 'can do' feeling motivated you, didn't it?

Now close your eyes and 'see' yourself in this positive mode. Notice how you looked, your body language, your smile!

Get right into the part again and recreate your go-getting mode. Make your visions as bright as you can, the bigger and more vivid your visualisation the more powerful its effect.

Now remember how you felt, get right into the skin of those upbeat and inspiring emotions. See and feel yourself reaching for and achieving your best.

Repeat this exercise whenever you need reminding of how good it can be for you. The more you can imagine yourself being in the flow, the easier it becomes to draw this reality into your life. Your energy attracts your circumstances, so get into the positive and inspirational flow of your own energy and the rest will just fall into place.

Keep practising this exercise.

108

JUST DO NOTHING

Weekends are too short – and now it's official. A survey by Thomson Holidays has shown that twenty-five per cent of holiday-makers are so stressed that it takes them forty-eight hours before they can start to relax!

The twenty-four-hour, twenty-first-century society means that we can all be on the go 24/7. But even busy bees stop buzzing after the sun has set! Not so very long ago, before electric lighting, people were forced to live at a slower pace and were more in tune with their own natural rhythms and the cycles of the seasons. But now our natural working day does not necessarily start at dawn and end at dusk – it can go on and on until we decide to stop, and some of us don't know *when* to stop.

Ten tips to help you to relax

1 Don't bring work home.

2 Create a real weekend and leave the answer machine on.

3 Turn off your mobile.

4 Remind yourself that your mind, body and soul *need* to relax.

5 Turn off the TV and have some quiet time.

6 Schedule some relaxation time in your diary.

7 Treat yourself to a massage.

8 Consciously slow down your breathing.

9 Don't fill every moment of your waking day; let there be some spaces where you can stand and stare and daydream.

10 Always remember that you are called a human *being* and not a human *doing* – learn to let yourself be.

Stop doing and start being.

109

INSPIRE YOURSELF

Twenty easy ways to feel inspired

1 Appreciate someone and tell them how you feel.

2 Do some activity that will calm your mind: yoga; t'ai chi; swimming; taking a sauna …

3 Follow your inspirational ideas.

4 Stand barefoot on the beach and inhale the ozone.

5 Start a conversation with a stranger.

6 Forgive someone.

7 Become absorbed by doing something that you love.

8 Buy some flowers for your desk at work.

9 Make a collage of your favourite photos.

10 Treat yourself to a new novel and curl up and read it … bliss!

11 Take the longer view and reflect upon

who you are becoming rather than what you are doing.

12 Perform an act of kindness (and keep it to yourself).

13 Make something (anything) and get those creative juices flowing.

14 Become aware of your hunches and gut feelings; are they trying to tell you something?

15 Listen to your favourite music (and do nothing else).

16 When in doubt, ask yourself what your heart feels.

17 Give something to someone.

18 Spend time having fun with a small child.

19 Write a letter to someone you love.

20 Pretend this is your last day on earth; make the most of it.

Act from your heart and be filled with inspiration.

110

GET REAL ABOUT LOVE

The romantic within us is a sucker for what are called the 'Love Myths'. These are the mistaken beliefs about the nature of true love, which lead us into making poor relationship choices, over and over again. If your relationships are a disaster zone you may recognise some of the following scenarios:

◆ If a partner is too nice you get bored.

◆ You just **knew** he was the one for you the moment you met.

◆ You need to give him your emotional support at all times.

◆ To feel truly in love you need drama and excitement.

◆ When the sex is great you know it's love.

◆ You stay a long time in a relationship that demoralises you because you think everything is your fault.

- The relationship is poor but you know he loves you really deep down because he is so full of remorse after he has treated you badly.

- You love to be in love and need to feel ecstatic in order to stay in a relationship.

- You put your partner on a pedestal and when he falls off you are disappointed in him.

Love Myths send us on a never-ending search for the perfect partner whom we will recognise immediately as the one who will fulfil our every need. Such is life in the movies and romantic fiction and many popular love songs; but this is not how it works in reality!

Understand how true intimacy works and let real love into your life.

111

MAKE GOOD VIBRATIONS

Your mind is a powerful energy broad-caster. Your thoughts are magnetic and they go out from you and draw to you those things that you think about. Think about how you feel when you spend time with someone who is extremely negative. The vibrations get very low and eventually affect your own mood. How do you feel when you spend time with someone who is positive and enthusiastic? The vibra-tions rise and you feel better for having met them. Your thoughts create your reality as they go out into the world and determine the events, people and objects that you attract into you life.

You can raise your energetic vibrations and feel lighter by using higher words and thoughts when you speak to yourself and to others. If you feel anxious or low use positive words to raise your energy. Say such words to yourself as: HARMONY, LOVE, PEACE, RADIANCE, BEAUTY, JOY,

ENTHUSIASM, COMMITTED, DELIGHT-FUL, INSPIRED ... Think and speak of all the beautiful and inspiring words you know. Notice how, when you use these words in conversation with other people, you will feel lighter and brighter. Use uplifting words in the company of others and watch and feel the changes in their energy and yours.

High words, high thoughts, high vibrations

This is a great exercise to do on the way to work. Take each letter of the alphabet and think of the highest, most positive word you can which begins with that letter.

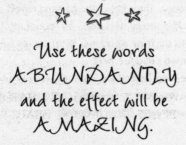

Use these words
ABUNDANTLY
and the effect will be
AMAZING.

112

KNOW YOURSELF

We are social creatures and our lives are rooted in the expectations, needs and aspirations of those around us. While we always need to be sensitive to the wishes of others, we must also be aware of our own needs. An optimistic, positive and upbeat approach always stems from a strong inner sense of self.

EXERCISE

Inner listening

Take regular time out to tune into your inner awareness (grab a moment in the office; on the Tube; in a taxi; in the shower ... wherever). Tap into your feelings throughout the day and reflect on what is happening. (*How do I feel about this? How does this decision affect me? What are my needs? Is this person good for me?*)

Make inner listening a 'must do' activity and you will find that your mind is less cluttered and that you have greater clarity in decision making. As you develop this technique you will start to create a calm inner space where you can think things through with a welcome sense of emotional detachment. Inner listening provides a platform where you can evaluate and test your feelings and ideas and this prevents you from overreacting to the daily dramas of life.

Give yourself time and space to get to know your real needs. Develop your reflective skills and others will find you more approachable and friendly.

Take the pressure off yourself and feel your levels of stress dropping away.

113

LOVE YOUR LIFE

Relax, close your eyes and steady your breathing. Let go of all your physical tension, let go of all your mental tension and feel yourself dropping into a calm place deep inside you.

As you sit quietly bring to mind all the simple things in your life that you love and appreciate. Some examples from clients are:

- ◆ the smell of roses
- ◆ freshly laundered sheets
- ◆ my mother's smile
- ◆ snow in the moonlight
- ◆ papers in bed on a Sunday morning
- ◆ Christmas carols
- ◆ Aunt Ellen's chocolate cake
- ◆ taking a sauna
- ◆ making sandcastles on the beach
- ◆ the hairs on the back of my baby's neck
- ◆ my best friend's laugh

- ◆ the smell of freshly ground coffee
- ◆ sitting in the sunshine
- ◆ taking my dog for a walk

Now open your eyes and write your own list. The wonderful thing about an appreciation list is that as soon as you start writing, more and more things come into your head. It's almost as if your feelings of appreciation and love open a door for all the good things in life to enter.

Reflect on your list and give thanks for all the gifts that you receive every day. Get into the love and appreciation habit and all aspects of your life will become more and more wonderful. Remember that you attract whatever you radiate.

Demonstrate love and appreciation and you will attract love and appreciation!

114

LIVE LIFE TO THE FULL

When you say or feel that you 'have to' do something it just takes all the joy out of the prospect, doesn't it? But when you become a person who 'wants to' do it, something magical happens in your life. In a recent interview, Oscar-winning actress Hilary Swank said that she has learned that she can do anything as long as she sets her mind to it. I was struck by her next comment: 'I don't do anything halfway.'

You will never, ever be happy if you do things halfway. When I was growing up my father used to say, 'If a thing is worth doing it's worth doing properly.' I didn't always appreciate his wisdom then but now I do, *and he is still saying it to me*! Thanks, Dad – it's good to be reminded.

What both Hilary and my dad are saying is: live life to the full! Why would we choose not to do this? Where is the joy in a half-hearted gesture?

If you are doing *anything* halfway ask yourself why. You might find that you are doing it to please someone else; if so it might be time to stop. There is no doubt that if you are living half-heartedly you will always be unhappy.

Choose to become an enthusiastic and a wholehearted 'want to' person, and if you really can't drop your 'have tos', *fake* some enthusiasm until you can feel it.

Get enthusiastic and notice how wonderful you feel.

115

ACHIEVE YOUR GOALS

If we have no goal how can we ever achieve anything? To lead a rich and full life we need to be able to mark our successes. It's all too easy to work hard towards something, and then, as we find ourselves coming close to our achievement, to subtly move the goalposts to ensure that we never actually score the goal. Have you ever done this? People who are only satisfied by perfection move their goalposts all the time and often find it hard to finish a project (it never seems to be quite good enough). Forget about being 'good enough': let go of your very high standards and make your goals realistic, achievable and rewardable.

Achieving my goals

1 Specify three short-term goals (achievable within three months).

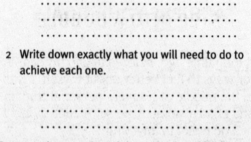

. . . .
. . . . , . . .
. . . .

2 Write down exactly what you will need to do to achieve each one.

. . . .
. . . .
. . . .

Focus on these goals and the action you will need to take to achieve them. Work towards your goals and don't change them as you get near to completion (no moving goalposts).

Allow yourself to achieve your goal (however modest you think it is). And then mark the achievement with a reward for yourself (make this real).

As you reach your short-term goals you will grow in confidence and know that you have it in you to make really great things happen!

116

STEP INTO A BUBBLE

A long time ago, before I began my search for ways to feel better about myself, I was in the middle of a severe personal trauma and I had absolutely no self-belief; in fact I had no belief in anything!

When we are in the depths of despair and suffer from low self-esteem we lose all sense of trust in ourselves and in other people, and so we feel lonely, vulnerable and afraid. This feeling of vulnerability can make us feel exposed and unprotected and very sensitive to others. While in this rather raw state I met someone who revealed to me a most amazing yet simple visualisation technique, which I used to strengthen and protect myself.

Create a bubble of light

Close your eyes and relax in a comfortable position and become aware of your breathing. Slowly follow your breaths in and out, in and out. Concentrate on the rhythm of your breathing until you are feeling very relaxed. Now imagine yourself standing in front of an open window. You see a beautiful bubble come floating through the window; notice its colour. It floats to the floor in front of you and, as you watch, it grows in size and beauty until it is bigger than you. Now step into your bubble. You are feeling totally protected and you know that nothing and no one can harm you when you are inside your beautiful bubble.

It only takes a moment to create this visualisation but it will leave you feeling totally protected and at ease.

117

RECEIVE AN ANGELIC BLESSING

EXERCISE

Making a set of Angelic Blessing cards

Transfer the words below on to paper or card, to make your own set of thirty Angelic Blessing cards. These cards provide key words that will help you to focus on particular aspects of your inner life.

SIMPLICITY	ENTHUSIASM	HEALING
FLEXIBILITY	SURRENDER	GRACE
SPONTANEITY	INSPIRATION	HONESTY
ADVENTURE	GRATITUDE	RESPONSIBILITY
HUMOUR	COURAGE	OPENNESS
TRUTH	WILLINGNESS	CLARITY
BEAUTY	HARMONY	CREATIVITY
COMPASSION	FORGIVENESS	TENDERNESS
FAITH	UNDERSTANDING	FREEDOM
LOVE	INTEGRITY	BALANCE

Find a quiet place and lay your cards face down in front of you. Relax and close your eyes and then turn your attention to a particular problem for which you need help. When you are ready choose a card; the one you select is the Angelic essence that you need to absorb at this time. Close your eyes again and absorb the qualities that this card brings. The Angel who represents this essence will be with you as you go about your business (I often take an Angel to work with me in my pocket). Think about the quality reflected in the card and as you do so you will find this quality reflected in all manner of ways throughout your day. Ask for an Angelic Blessing and choose a card whenever you feel the need.

Strengthen your divine connection and amazing things will happen.

118

HELP YOURSELF

You can read every self-help book in the universe and still not be able to change your life; you can attend personal development workshops and still feel stuck; you can meditate to clear your mind and still not be able to clear up your problems. It's quite possible to become a self-help junkie: addicted to the *idea* of change and still looking for answers in the outer world (books, teachers, gurus, counsellors, therapies, coaches).

In times of difficulty we all seek opinions, validation, guidance and support from others; this is how we gather information, look for new directions and begin making life-changing decisions. But our search can actually become an end in itself. If you have a shelf of self-help books and *still* feel that you can't help yourself then maybe it's time to begin, right now!

There is a huge chasm between knowledge and experience. If you read all the tips in this book but didn't use any of them they could never work for you. Similarly you could invest your coach/ friend/parent with more power to understand you than you have yourself. This could never be the true state of affairs; no one else can know the real you.

While wise guidance is helpful, it is only valuable in as much as you can resonate with its meaning and take appropriate action on your own behalf. No one can think, believe, feel or act for you.

Your life is your own and only you can know what's right for you.

119

BE A WINNER AT WORK

Ten winning workplace strategies

1 **Get known for your reliability**: finish tasks and get to meetings on time.

2 **Be friendly with everyone you meet** and get to know their names; others will respond positively and remember who you are.

3 **Set deadlines that are realistic**, and even overestimate the time you might need. If you get it done before the deadline you will look super-efficient.

4 **Let others know of your achievements**. Managers who know their job will be more impressed by your successes than by the hours that you put in.

5 **Look self-assured**. As fifty-five per cent of your impact comes through non-verbal communication make sure your body language is confident, smile and maintain good eye contact.

6 **Sound enthusiastic**. Look interested and be interested.

7 **Make sure your work area is clutter-free** and have a beautiful plant or fresh flowers on your desk. The impression you give will be ordered yet creative.

8 **Remember your colleagues' birthdays** with a small token. Workplace rituals help to bring people together.

9 **Be seen as a team player** and always support others' efforts. Develop good relationships at work and the atmosphere will be much happier.

10 **Network and let people know what you are doing**. Your work contacts are the most likely gateway to promotion or a new career opportunity.

You take your own mood to work; remember that positivity gets results.

120

PUT YOUR HEART INTO IT

We do not always feel brimming with the love of the universe. Life throws many challenges our way and on such a day we still have to make important decisions and choices.

Sometimes we act out of fear instead of love: perhaps we behave badly towards someone to cause them pain; find ourselves unable to express our true feelings or just float off course so that we don't fulfil our commitments. So it is easy to find that we have become half-hearted about life and are drifting into negativity, depression, boredom and low self-esteem.

As soon as you begin to feel less than your best, recognise your symptoms and then check the true nature of your present path. When you are living wholeheartedly: you feel good; relationships are support-ive; you feel positive and enthusiastic (even if things don't always go perfectly) and there is an overall awareness that you are 'going with the flow'.

Take any challenging area of your life (we all have these) and check for the above points. Apply this procedure to any part of your life that feels unhappy and remember: if your heart is not in it, your life will never feel worth living.

- ◆ Ask yourself some searching questions.
- ◆ Challenge your own behaviour and actions: why are you being untrue to yourself?
- ◆ Seek some answers; be true to yourself.
- ◆ Take courage.
- ◆ Commit yourself wholeheartedly.

As soon as you put your heart into it, your life will take off.

121

BELIEVE THAT YOU DESERVE THE BEST

If your energy is feeling 'stuck' and your positive affirmations and visualisations don't seem to be working any more, it might be time to check on your beliefs about 'deservability'. If you don't believe that you deserve the best then you will never allow good things into your life.

EXERCISE

Discovering what you think you deserve

1 What do you deserve?

....

Do you think that you deserve to fulfil your dreams?

Do you deserve the best that life has to offer?

Do you believe that you don't deserve very much or, in fact, nothing at all?

2   Why are you a deserving person? or

3   Why are you not a deserving person?

Answer whichever question you think applies to you.

Closely examine your beliefs about what you think you deserve. Where have these beliefs come from? What did your parents say about what you deserved? Did you deserve a good clip around the ear or a good telling-off? What did your parents think that they deserved? Did they feel that they deserved the good things in life? Perhaps they were disappointed by life; maybe they felt that they didn't get what they deserved. Think about all the 'deserving' messages you may have received, whether spoken to you or picked up in more subtle ways.

Believe that you deserve the best, because you do!

122

MAKE YOUR POSITIVE AFFIRMATIONS

Our self-esteem is based on our self-belief and when the going gets rough it is often difficult to maintain our belief in our self.

If we are blue it feels impossible to believe that we are special, worthy and lovable. But of course it is always true. It is at these times of difficulty that we most need to believe in ourselves. Belief is strong magic!

When it feels impossible to love yourself, then practise. Practise believing that you are amazing, important, wonderful, creative, deserving and significant – because you are.

Your positive affirmations

Create your own list of affirming self-beliefs. Keep these affirmations in the present tense; keep them positive and practise saying them all the time. Refer to your list as soon as you feel your self-esteem dropping away. Use the examples below if you wish and create some more of your own.

Examples

I love and value myself

I am a wonderful and creative person

I deserve the best in life

MY LIST OF POSITIVE AFFIRMATIONS

1 ....

2 ....

3 ....

You are always special, worthy and lovable.

123

THINK BEAUTIFUL THOUGHTS

Thoughts are powerful things; whatever you put your attention to will grow. Imagine that your mind is a garden. You can fill your mind with beautiful flowers or let it become overgrown and out of control with weeds. We can't have two opposing thoughts at the same time, so if you are holding a positive thought there will be no room for a negative one.

Actively plant positive seeds in the garden of your mind and weed out any negatives as soon as they appear. As soon as you become aware of a negative entering your mind, nip it in the bud. Then think of its opposite and form a good positive mental picture; let this replace the negative. It might take a while to recognise your negatives (they come in many disguises and you may have been comfortable with them all your life). As you actively plant positive seeds in your mind you will find it easier to recognise the negative intruders.

Replacing negatives

- If you feel angry, think the biggest loving thought that you can. By accentuating the positive you automatically eliminate the negative; there's no room for both thoughts.

- If you feel rushed, stop, close your eyes and visualise a beautiful calm scene.

- If you feel like a loser repeat the affirmation 'I am a winner'.

When we can fill our minds with beautiful thoughts our world becomes a beautiful place.

124

LISTEN TO YOUR INTUITION

EXERCISE

Relax and listen

- Take some time every day, even if it's only a few minutes, to tune into your intuition. Find a quiet spot where you won't be interrupted, close your eyes and relax your body. Breathe deeply and slowly and relax your mind. If your thoughts intrude just let them go and bring your concentration back to your breathing. In this relaxed and quiet state you can allow your intuition to come through.

- Be prepared to 'hear' it in any number of different ways. Some people recognise their voice and others don't have any immediate awareness. You may experience strong feelings or you may not. One of the best ways to make your connection is to ask your intuition for guidance in a particular matter.

- Make your question as specific as possible and then let go of all preconceived ideas of how you expect your answers to come.

- Give yourself some quiet time so that your intuition can focus on your dilemma.

- Then, when you have finished, let go of all thoughts about this matter.

Your inner guidance can come at any time and in any shape or form; the words of a song; a book open at a certain page; a chance meeting; a strong feeling to act in a certain way ... so let your mind stay open to all possibilities.

When you hear the message of your inner voice, you will just know what to do.

125

TAP INTO RICH ENERGY

When you are feeling prosperous you are positive, generous and upbeat and you radiate feelings of trust, open-heartedness and abundance. What is it that brings you this personal sense of satisfaction? Are you rich in friendships, love, health, awareness, success, abilities, interests ...?

Prosperity consciousness surrounds you with 'rich energy', which magnetises even more positive outcomes (you attract whatever you radiate). Appreciate all that you have and recognise the abundance of good things in the universe and every aspect of your life will dramatically improve.

If you are experiencing any deficiency in your life it's only too easy to blame it on lack of money. But think again: you know that money can't buy the qualities that bring you happiness. If you feel impoverished it means that you are not getting enough of what you want, whether it's love, attention, success, confidence, money or whatever. What is it that you feel you lack?

Scarcity consciousness and a negative fear-based outlook will create an aura of 'poor energy' around you and this will attract a sense of shortage and lack into every corner of your life (including your finances).

Change your 'poor energy' to 'rich energy' by affirming prosperity consciousness instead of scarcity consciousness. Back hope instead of hopelessness, go for beliefs that make you feel good, affirm prosperity and it will be yours. Embrace the benevolent energy of the universe.

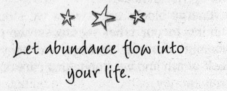

Let abundance flow into
your life.

126

LISTEN TO YOUR BODY

Because we exist at the mental, spiritual, physical and emotional levels, our personal healing always involves balancing these parts of ourselves. When we *are* balanced, our energies are flowing freely; they are in harmony and we are 'at ease'. If for some reason there is a block in the circuit, then we become out of balance, we are *dis*-eased (not at ease) and eventually we become ill in some way.

Your own healing rests ultimately with you. Only you can know what you need for your own mental, emotional, spiritual and physical health.

Energy blocks arise when we stop listening to our inner messages; we don't support our true feelings; we deny our self-worth and we stop taking care of ourselves.

Whenever you are ill, your body is trying to tell you something. Rest and listen to its messages. Why are you ill? Are you holding negative beliefs about yourself? What are your symptoms telling you about your thoughts, expectations and lifestyle? Try this exercise:

Making positive affirmations for health

Make any of the following affirmations as often as you can. Write them, say them, sing them. Surround yourself with healing consciousness and feel your energy respond.

I deserve vibrant health

I love and value myself

I love my body

I am ready to be well now

I can heal myself

I trust my inner messages

It is safe to be well

When your body is telling you something, stop and listen to it.

127

BREATHE FOR CONFIDENCE

Most people take twelve to eighteen breaths per minute, which is incredible when you consider this amazing fact: *when we breathe eight breaths a minute, or fewer, our entire metabolism changes and we become relaxed, confident and capable. We are perceived as authoritative and charismatic and we feel it!*

EXERCISE

The basic breath

Sit on the edge of a chair with your back straight and feet on the floor. Hold your hands around your lower abdomen, one each side of your stomach.

Exhale fully with a loud sigh. Deflate your stomach down to your groin and hold it empty for a few seconds.

Start to inhale very slowly, with your mouth closed and feel your lower abdomen swelling in your hands. Visualise the area from your groin to your ribcage as a beautiful coloured balloon and watch and feel it inflate slowly, filling from the bottom (imagine the air coming from between your legs). Expand your balloon fully and hold for three seconds.

Exhale slowly, watching the balloon deflate, until your abdomen is flat.

Repeat for five complete breaths.

These steps form the basis of slow and complete breathing – natural breathing. You will experience the benefits of this exercise after only a few minutes. Keep practising daily and very soon you will be down to eight breaths a minute. Eventually your everyday breathing patterns will change and you will find yourself experiencing new levels of confidence and self-awareness.

Slow down your breathing and feel the difference.

128

IMAGINE YOUR DREAM JOB

When you can really visualise a goal you start a magical process which brings that goal nearer and nearer to becoming a reality. Whatever you focus upon will become true for you in some way: **seeing** leads to **believing** and this makes you so much closer to **creating** your vision. So why not visualise, believe and create your dream job?

Relax and close your eyes. Slow down your breathing and let go of any tension in your body.

Imagine your perfect job. See the environment in as much detail as possible. Do you work alone or do you have colleagues? What type of people are they?

See yourself travelling to work. How do you get there? What are you wearing and how do you feel? Make this fantasy as real as you can and put yourself in the very centre of the picture.

If you are in an office see it as clearly as

possible. If you are a teacher see the classroom, if you are a landscape gardener see the garden, if you are a hairdresser see the salon …

Really get into the skin of this perfect job and feel your happiness and contentment. See yourself smiling and having a good time. Notice how confident and relaxed you are feeling and how friendly your colleagues are. Bring your fantastic dream job into full colour and hear the soundtrack. *Make it as real as you can!*

When you open your eyes just remind yourself that you are one step closer to your perfect job, because you are!

129

REPLACE 'SHOULD' WITH 'COULD'

Write down all the things that you think you should be doing.

Examples

I should lose weight

I should be more positive

I should read a lot more

Now take each 'I should' from your list, read it out loud and then ask yourself, 'Why should I?' Voicing your feelings helps your understanding. Write down your answers; you might be surprised by what you have written.

Examples

Because I'm too lazy/stupid/careless/ worthless/fat … etc.

Because people might not like me the way I am.

Because my father said I should.

The answers to 'Why should I?' questions show us how we can limit ourselves by holding certain beliefs. 'Should' implies reluctance and also indicates feelings of guilt and fear. Whenever you think or say that you 'should' or 'ought to' do some-thing, recognise that you are putting yourself in the wrong in some way. Rewrite your list replacing 'should' with 'could' and start each statement with, 'If I really wanted to'. For example: *if I really wanted to I could read a lot more.*

When you rewrite your list in this way you might find that there are some things that you don't even want to change.

*Don't be a 'should' victim
trapped by guilt.
Why not allow yourself the
possibility of 'could'?*

130

LET GO OF THE PAST

Consider this list:

- ◆ Because he let me down I can never trust another man.

- ◆ Because I was bullied at school I can't make friends now.

- ◆ Because I failed that exam I can't learn anything new.

- ◆ Because my parents criticised me I can never feel confident.

- ◆ Because I don't believe in God I cannot develop my spirituality.

- ◆ Because I did something that was wrong I deserve to be punished forever.

  - ◆ Because I think that I am stupid I can't train for a new job.

And so it can go, on and on and on … The truth is that holding on to the past (however terrible it was) serves no purpose except to carry on hurting us. Where are you hanging on to the past?

What are you hanging on to?

Imagine that you are holding a gigantic magnifying glass in front of your life. What can you see that you couldn't see before? What or whom have you outgrown? Think about the following categories:

  negative thoughts

  victim behaviour (being a doormat)

  rescuing behaviour (being a saviour)

  pessimism

  unequal relationships (bullied or bullying)

  low self-belief

  anger (festering)

  denial (head in the sand)

  sadness

Look through this list and see if it gives you any inspiration. You are looking for the clues that might lead you to a solution. As soon as you recognise something that you are hanging on to, name it.

And now decide to let go of whatever holds you back.

131

SEARCH FOR THE HERO INSIDE YOURSELF

Who do you most admire? Who are your own personal heroes and heroines? These people might be media celebrities, sports personalities or your friend up the road who is so good at keeping positive in spite of all her problems. Make a list of your heroes and write down exactly why you admire them.

EXERCISE

Become your hero

Now take one of your heroes and visualise him/her doing or being whatever it is that you most admire. Close your eyes and imagine walking right up to this person and stepping into their shoes. Imagine having the gifts and qualities that this person has. Let yourself 'be' this person for a few moments before you come back to yourself.

Look carefully at the qualities that you most admire in your list of people. At some level you already have these qualities. If you can recognise certain strengths in others then you must also be aware of the capacity for these in yourself (otherwise you would never have recognised them).

You are so much more than you think you are. However ordinary you imagine your life to be, the truth is that you have been given magical gifts: the ability to love, care, transform, sympathise, create, achieve ...

Search for the hero inside yourself who is able to use these gifts to create a full and incredible life.

132

ATTRACT MORE MONEY

If you want to attract more money, start by looking at your beliefs. If you worry about money you will find yourself in a downward spiral of poverty and deprivation. When you send out negative messages ('I have no money', 'I am poor', 'I can't pay the bills'...) then your unconscious will support your beliefs and keep manifesting this reality for you. You will get more of what you are affirming, and in this case that means less and less money.

So check your money beliefs. What are your thoughts drawing into your life? Your deep beliefs about money can make or break you financially. For example, if you thought that money was unclean or that it might compromise you in some way then it's unlikely that you will ever be able to let it flow into your life; you would be too worried about its bad influence. And if at some level you don't believe that you deserve much then you will always stay trapped in your 'poor energy' (receiving only as much as you think you deserve).

So instead of worrying about not having enough and asking, 'What will I do without enough money?', get creative and ask yourself, 'What can I do to create more money?'

Take a look at the real state of your finances, check your spending and saving habits, plug a few money drains and you will immediately find yourself feeling more empowered and in control of the money in your life.

Money flows to those who love it.

133

APPRECIATE WHAT OTHERS BRING

Relax, close your eyes and become aware of your breathing. Let all thoughts drift away as you focus on this visualisation.

Circle of love visualisation

Imagine yourself at the centre of a circle of people.

You recognise everyone in the circle as someone who is or has been very close to you. Let your circle include your family, lovers and close friends. Each person in this circle will be meaningful to you.

Look at each one in turn and ask yourself, 'What gift did this person bring me?'

Let each person step forward one at a time and give you their gift.

It doesn't matter if you don't know what it is; just take what they hand you and smile and thank them. Go right round your circle collecting your gifts.

This is your circle of love and everyone here has come into your life for a very important reason; they have each come to teach you something of great significance about yourself. When all the gifts are at your feet, dissolve your circle and come out of the visualisation.

You may already have recognised some, many or none of your gifts but eventually you will recognise them all. Remember that not all gifts come gift-wrapped! Some come in disguise as problems or challenges, and they offer you the unique opportunity to develop your strength and to overcome them.

Be thankful to everyone for
the gifts they bring.

134

TAKE YOUR DAY ONE STEP AT A TIME

Sometimes it's hard to find the energy to get up and out. You might have a lot on your mind; you may have a busy schedule; there might be difficulties to face. When your day gets off to a difficult start try this exercise.

EXERCISE

Taking one step at a time

Concentrate on the immediate task in hand. Just get yourself out of bed before you think of the next job. *Take one step at a time.* Don't think about the next step until the immediate stage is over. Each time you achieve one step, stop and congratulate yourself. In this way every small task becomes an achievement, which indeed it is on a day when the going is tough. By refusing to be drawn into worrying about the rest of the day you protect yourself from going down a negative spiral which can begin with such thoughts as: *Oh, how am I ever going to get to that meeting; pick up the children; do the shopping; cook the dinner?... I'll never manage it all.*

As you achieve more and more tasks (congratulating yourself along the way) your view of the day will become much more positive and you will start to feel in control again. There is a fine feeling of accomplishment when we lift ourselves up in the face of adversity and one step at a time is the only way to do it.

Celebrate every small accomplishment and soon you will feel back in control.

135

GET OUT OF THAT RUT

EXERCISE

Deciding to change

Think of a situation where you feel stuck and unsure.

Describe the problem.

What exactly would you like to change?

Describe your new ideal situation (in as much detail as possible).

What part did you play in helping to create this difficult situation? Look objectively at your behaviour. Have you been honest about your feelings? Have you been clear about where you stand?

What is the first step that you would need to take to start changing the present situation?

What attitudes or beliefs would you need to change in order to take this first step? In other words, what are the negative patterns that have helped to create the original problem?

Change is easy; it all begins with you. Your habits

are only learned behaviours – they are not set in stone (although this may sometimes feel very hard to believe).

We become what we practise most, so watch what you are practising. Accept responsibility for the quality of your life and focus on what you want rather than what you don't want. Believe in yourself and your capacity to change and know that you can break all your inhibiting habits and patterns.

As you reach beyond your old limitations you will feel a remarkable increase in your energy and your confidence and life will become more interesting and expansive.

Get out of that rut and start buzzing again.

136

RECOGNISE WORKAHOLISM

Workaholics are quite easy to spot once you know the symptoms – they make their lives and the lives of others miserable – so check the following characteristics to see if you are working for one or you live with one, or even if you are one!

Workaholic checklist

◆ Nothing is ever good enough.

◆ Takes on everything that comes up.

◆ Hates delegating.

◆ Poor social life.

◆ Critical and short-tempered with subordinates.

◆ Considerable desire to please bosses.

◆ Compulsive doer. Can't relax.

◆ No interest in casual chat.

◆ Loves routine.

◆ Takes everything seriously.

- ◆ Has a backlog of unused holiday time.
- ◆ Poor communication skills.
- ◆ Lack of emotional understanding; is distant with others.
- ◆ Gets things out of proportion, no sense of the bigger picture.

If you are working with or for a workaholic then you will definitely be feeling stressed. If your partner is one then your home life will be affected. And if you are one, recognise the symptoms and begin to let some **real life** into your life.

Work can be fun, creative and inspiring, but it stops being all these things if we take it too seriously.

137

CULTIVATE YOUR SELF-ESTEEM

On a bad day, when we are low in self-esteem and spiralling rapidly down into a pit of negativity, we see a world where everyone is clever/getting things together/having amazing relationships/coping easily with stress ... Of course the rest of the world is not really like this, it's just the way it seems when we feel out of control.

All human beings struggle with self-esteem issues – yes, even those oh-so-confident-looking folk. It seems as if our self-esteem is always on the line. We can go up and down and up and down again with alarming speed. (Does this sound like you?) Take heart, all of us are working on our self-esteem.

Our self-esteem is rather like a beautiful but delicate flower and it needs constant nourishment and care in order for it to grow and remain protected. Use any of the tips in this book that will help you to pull yourself out of negativity and increase your good feelings about yourself.

Always remember that whenever you are working on your self-esteem you are focusing on your own personal development. You are not alone; this job is a lifetime's work (and joy!). Don't get depressed about losing your self-esteem – it happens to all of us, all of the time. However, as you cultivate ways to bring positive changes into your life, your self-esteem will become more stable.

Next time when you feel dispirited you will be able to pick yourself up, dust yourself down and start all over again.

138

KNOW WHAT SORT OF LOVER YOU ARE

It takes two to tango, so let's take a realistic look at what you bring to your relationship. If you are not with a partner at the moment then think about how you thought, felt and behaved in a previous relationship. Complete the following statements.

I show my love by . . . .

I am disappointed when he . . . .

I can't forgive him when . . . .

My worst characteristic is . . . .

I tend to feel clingy when . . . .

I feel secure in a relationship when . . . . .

I feel insecure when . . . .

When I feel confident our relationship looks . . . .

When I feel low in confidence it looks . .

One of the mistakes I have made is . . . . .

I expect him to . . . .

When he doesn't fulfil my expectations I

Our sex life is . . . .

I feel sexy when . . . .

Love is . . . .

Our best moments are . . . .

I can forgive . . . .

Long-term relationships feel . . . .

The most positive thing about us is . . . . .

I am attracted to him because . . . .

Think about the part you play in your intimate relationships. What strengths, weaknesses and needs do your statements reveal about you?

You attract the love relationships that reflect your deepest beliefs and emotions.

139

DO WHATEVER TURNS YOU ON

You can easily change the way you feel without indulging in mood enhancers or comfort food. Think how easily the simple things in life can alter your emotions. Perhaps a certain piece of music can lift you, a walk, a piece of artwork, sex, a poem, surfing, driving, cooking, swimming, dancing, shopping, singing ... there are numerous possibilities here. Start to notice whatever changes your mood for the better.

Some years ago when I was working on creative projects with students I discovered something that really turns me on. When I went to a stationery shop to buy coloured card and pens for my classes I felt energised and excited by all the creative possibilities that the shop offered. As I gazed at fluorescent paper and board markers I felt an unmistakeable surge of excitement as my imagination began to run riot. Each time I went to buy stationery items I came away buzzing with new ideas. Now, I often just wander around the stationery departments just to experience this creative lift. We all get turned on and inspired by very different things, and they are most often the simple things in life.

The things that turn me on

Spend the next couple of days really thinking about what it is that energises and excites you. Then write your list:

- ....
- ....
- ....

Now do these things!

Do something that you love and just feel that amazing positive energy flowing through you.

140

STOP STRESSING ABOUT STRESS

Newspapers and magazines are forever telling us that 'stress kills', and feed us with frightening statistics that prove that stress is the main cause of terrifying illnesses. A huge stress reduction industry has been built providing books; therapies; courses; relaxation classes; fitness centres ... all to help us de-stress. Let's lighten up and stop blaming stress for all our worries, as if it's an illness with a cure. There's no need to be afraid of becoming stressed (and so making ourselves more stressed). *Stress is only a word that is used to describe the feelings we have when we are not coping very well with our lives.*

Getting it together

The next time you think you are suffering with stress, do the following:

1 Stop worrying about what stress will do to you. Recognise that you are only experiencing a feeling of being unable to cope.

2 Ask yourself if you can do anything to resolve the situation. If you can't, then accept this and let go of the worry. If you can, then make an action plan.

3 Discover what needs doing. Make a list of the practical steps you need to take. Then **ACT!** Take each step as it comes and work your way through this dilemma.

Stop worrying about your stress levels and just do what needs to be done. You have all the ability you need to cope with whatever life throws at you.

Positive action is the antidote to stress.

141

LOOK FOR THE SILVER LINING

Life is full of ups and downs and we can learn from everything that happens to us. So, a stable relationship ends; we fail an exam; lose a job ... Once the initial anger/dependency/depression is over we can review our setbacks and use them to learn more about ourselves. Every event in our lives has a purpose; there is a powerful intention in every situation. Rather than remaining in a negative state, which will only take you further down, try approaching the situation in a new way.

EXERCISE

Finding the silver lining

Ask yourself the following questions:
- How did this happen?
- How can I see this situation differently?
- In what way can this loss work for me?
- What can I learn about myself here?

- **What is there that is positive in this situation?**

If this is hard to do, think back to a difficult time in the past. For example, you may have lost a job opportunity and so found yourself taking a totally different direction which turned out to be exactly 'right' for you. An intimate relationship may have ended leaving you heartbroken. Perhaps this relationship wasn't good for you and you only see this as your heart mends and you start to enjoy your new freedom and independence. As one door closes another opens.

Look for the newly opening door; look for the silver lining.

142

STAND UP FOR YOURSELF

A non-victim response is an assertive response. We are assertive when we:

Act in our own best interests and stand up for ourselves.

Communicate our needs clearly and also respect the rights and feelings of other people.

Value ourselves and others.

EXERCISE

Change your victim behaviour

Think of a situation where you know you are being victimised.

1 The situation is:

. . . .

Describe the ways that you behave in this situation.

2 I behave like a victim by:

. . . .

What messages are you conveying about your
thoughts and feelings surrounding this
situation?

3 I show the following thoughts and feelings:

   . . . .

   Why are you not demonstrating your true
   feelings and needs in this situation?

4 What is the worst thing that can happen if I
   stand up for myself?

   . . . .

Go back to your victimising situation and change
the script. By taking an assertive role how could
you change your answers to Question 2?

*Stop being a victim, and stand
up for yourself.*

143

DEVELOP RELATIONSHIP CONFIDENCE

Wherever you go you take yourself and this is never so obvious as when you enter a relationship. Whatever the initial sexual chemistry between you, the quality of your relationship will depend exactly upon your levels of personal self-confidence. However much you fancy him it will not work unless you both **think, feel** and **act confidently.**

When you **think confidently** you believe in yourself and trust your instincts. You know that you deserve to be treated with the utmost respect and you have a positive and optimistic approach to your relationship. You are open to changes and you think that you both have an equally important role in your partnership. You know what you want from the relationship.

When you are **feeling confident** you have a strong sense of inner stability and security. You are in touch with your emotions and are not afraid to show your partner that you care. You love to give and receive spontaneous acts of affection and you expect to be appreciated.

When you **act confidently** you are dependable and reliable and you can be decisive and effective. You are not afraid to take risks and you have good open communication skills. You expect your partner to be trustworthy and to share his thoughts and feelings with you.

A truly intimate relationship is one where both partners have the confidence to be themselves and feel free to disclose their pain as well as their pleasure.

Express your confidence and just watch your relationships improve.

144

RELAX, RELAX, RELAX ...

Sit comfortably, close your eyes and become aware of your breathing. As your mind fills with numerous thoughts just notice them and let them go. Don't follow your thoughts (they will keep coming, your mind never stops).

Instead, come back to your breathing. Follow your in breaths and out breaths: in and out, in and out, and as you do so start to become aware of your body.

Now imagine that your whole body is relaxing. Begin with your toes and feel a great wave of relaxation sweeping through your feet, calves and thighs. You can feel your legs getting heavier and heavier.

Let this calm and relaxed feeling travel up into your abdomen and lower back. Feel the warm peaceful energy move into your chest, upper back and shoulders. As you let your shoulders droop your body is very heavy, warm, relaxed and peaceful.

Let go of all tension in your hands, arms, neck, head and face. As you feel your facial muscles letting go your jaws and eyes feel heavy and relaxed.

You are now completely comfortable and at ease and a wonderful feeling of peace and serenity surrounds you. Enjoy!

When you are ready come back slowly into the room. This is a great routine for any time when you need to let go of the stresses and strains of the day.

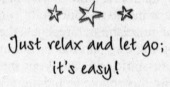

Just relax and let go;
it's easy!

145

CALM YOUR MIND

We know how to satisfy our material desires by going out into the world and experiencing things, feeling things and doing things. However, if we live our lives only at the material level we will eventually feel disenchanted.

All the possessions, friends and abilities in the world do not compensate for a lack of spiritual connection. Don't forget that you are mind, body and spirit, and that spiritual nourishment reaches the parts that nothing else can reach. Get in touch with your spirit and calm your mind and body with this simple technique.

EXERCISE

Easy meditation

1 Find a quiet and peaceful place and sit in a comfortable chair so that your back remains straight.

2 Close your eyes and begin to watch your

mind. Let your thoughts come and observe them. Don't get involved with your thoughts; just notice them.

3 When you are ready, turn your attention to your breathing. Notice the muscle in your abdomen, just below your ribcage, which rises and falls as you breathe. Follow its movement. Each time the muscle rises, think 'rising' and every time it falls, think 'falling'.

4 Rising ... falling ... rising ... falling; let all your other thoughts drift away as you focus on this muscle. At first your mind will keep wandering off and each time it does just follow it and bring it back to focusing on 'rising ... falling ... rising ...'

Keep practising; it *will* get easier.

☆ ☆ ☆

A calm mind is a priceless reward.

146

LOOK AT THE BIGGER PICTURE

The bigger picture of your life shows you *why* things are happening to you, why you have been led in a certain direction and how these situations and experiences have been absolutely necessary for you to complete a future stage of your life.

EXERCISE

Draw your lifeline

Take a large sheet of paper and draw your lifeline. Start at birth and draw a line that represents the important ups and downs in your life. This line doesn't have to be to scale or be a work of art, but do make a note of significant points. I have used this technique many times in workshops and people always experience new personal insights and revelations as they look at the bigger picture of the events in their lives.

If I hadn't met her then I never would have ... I took that decision then never realising how it would affect me all these years later ... Who would have guessed how that period of depression would have led me to a turning point in my career ...? When that relationship ended I was distraught, but with hindsight I think it was the best thing that could have happened to me ...

Look for the connections and meaningful coincidences in your own lifeline. Search for the link between cause and effect and see the synchronicity at work in your life. When you connect with the bigger picture you will receive insights and revelations that will help you to see the reasons why certain things have happened to you.

The details of your life have
meaning and purpose.

147

OVERCOME YOUR ADDICTIONS

We can be addicted to so many things: abusive relationships; overeating; under-eating; drinking; drugs (illegal or prescribed); smoking; overworking; over-spending; overexercising ... the list is endless. If we are compulsively using any behaviour to hide from our true feelings and to punish ourselves, then we are addicted. Some addictions are life-threat-ening and others threaten the quality of our life. If you are involved in any self-harming behaviour then you will know it.

EXERCISE

Letting go of your addictions

Write down your answers to this exercise.

Assess your situation. Describe your relationship with your addiction.

Decide what you would like to change. What don't you like about your condition?

State your preferred outcome. How do you want things to change? Be specific.

Recognise why you have become addicted. Deep self-hatred; the need to fill the emptiness inside; fear of anger; lack of trust; desire to be in control; a need to punish yourself and lack of self-forgiveness are some of the things that may have brought you here. Once you can see the roots of your addiction you are on the way to recovery.

Seek help. Find a counsellor and/or a support group or any other suitably qualified professional who can help you. Look on the Internet and find others who are going through the same thing as you.

No person and no thing has any power over you, unless you give them that power.

148

LOVE YOUR ENEMIES

This is such a powerful technique so please don't give up before you've given it a chance.

Make a list of all those people who you can't stand. If there's no one on your list, turn to the next page; however, I expect that you have some names. We all struggle with human relationships and unless we have achieved saintly perfection we will inevitably become irritated and angry with certain people in our lives.

Interestingly, the things that we find most annoying in others are often the qualities that we are struggling with ourselves (that is why we are so irritated).

Choose someone from your list and ask yourself the following questions:

◆ Why *exactly* does this person irritate me so much? Look beneath the surface of your feelings.

◆ Does their behaviour mirror mine in any way?

◆ Is it worth continually winding myself up with angry thoughts just so that I can go on hating them?

EXERCISE

Last day on earth forgiveness

When you next meet a person on your list imagine that it is their last day on earth and that you will never see them again. Take this chance to change the nature of your relationship.

Forgiveness is hard but possible.

Forgiveness makes you feel
FANTASTIC
— it's worth all the hard work and the gifts it brings are the greatest we can receive.

149

DRAW YOUR LINE IN THE SAND

Imagine that someone needs your help. They want you to do something for them but you have already made plans with someone else. What will you do? If you say 'yes' and abandon your own plans, are you being a good friend or are you being a victim? And if you have ever felt overwhelmed by someone else's feelings or swamped by a partner in an intimate relationship then you will have felt similarly compromised.

Sometimes it can be very hard to decide whether your needs come before or after the needs of someone else. Every situation is different, but there is a process that you can use to help you to decide exactly how far you will go for another person, or in other words where you will draw your own line in the sand.

Are you being victimised?

Check that you are acting from the best possible
motives and not because you are allowing yourself
to be victimised.

- Review the situation and your feelings.

- If you are saying 'yes' but you experience
  fear, anger, intimidation, resentment,
  irritation, helplessness or low self-esteem,
  then it is time for you to draw a new line in the
  sand.

- Create a new boundary line – I will go this far
  and no further.

*Remember that you can be a
good friend/lover/colleague
. . . and still say 'no'.*

150

STAY INTERESTED

Do something different, something you have never done before. Go to a concert to hear some music that is new to you; sign up for a pottery class; eat vegetarian food; learn a new language; visit a place where you have never been ... The possibilities are endless. When we do something for the first time we always experience a change of energy and we learn something new about ourselves.

Looking for something new encourages our natural curiosity, inquisitiveness and awareness. Young children have a natural interest in anything they haven't experienced before; they purposefully pursue new activities because this is how they learn about their world.

Unfortunately as we grow older we lose this wide-eyed passionate interest in life, and low confidence levels can bring boredom and fatigue. Re-awaken your interest by seeking a new experience and/or try the following exercise.

Expand your comfort zone

- What did you love to do ten years ago that you don't do now?

- Which of these things would you like to do again?

- Why have you stopped doing the things you love?

- Go back another ten years and repeat this exercise.

- Go back as far as you can.

- Now choose one thing from your list and DO IT.

- How do you feel? Choose another one and another one ...

Keep interested and fascinated by life and your energy and enthusiasm will soar.

151

EXPECT A MIRACLE

Some years ago when I was running a class for unemployed youngsters I asked them what they thought they needed to help them to get a job and wrote whatever they said next to their name. We had things like more training, educational qualifications, better communication skills, computer knowledge ... And then I reached a young man who said that he had a police record and that he would 'need a miracle'.

I told him to go home and to start believing that miracles do happen. Within a week he had applied for a job that was advertised nationally. Through an incredible set of circumstances and in the face of tough competition he got that job, quit the class and we were all left speechless.

Miracles are love in action and if you don't believe in them they will never happen to you. We can attract miracles into our lives but only if we truly believe they are possible. Forget about not *really* allowing yourself to believe in case you are disappointed. Fear of disappointment will stand in your way forever! You are disappointed anyway, what have you got to lose?

Expect a miracle for a week. Wholeheartedly believe that one will happen and keep trusting. The miracle might not be the one you were expecting but I can assure you that *something amazing* will happen.

Belief is the most powerful
magic of all.

152

GIVE UP THE WORRYING HABIT

While we look to the material world to fulfil all our needs we will never be truly happy. Once we are adequately fed, clothed and sheltered we must look beyond the 'things' of the world if we are to be fulfilled and content (more clothes, more food, bigger houses will not do it for us).

We are looking for much more than material gifts. We need: spiritual and emotional fulfilment; to feel a sense of connection with each other and with the natural world; to have an underlying sense of meaning and purpose to our days and to feel deep appreciation for the miracle which is our life. We are bigger than our worries and we don't have to succumb to the dreaded 'stress'; we only need to look inside ourselves to discover the happiness we seek.

A day of peace and tranquillity

Give up the worrying habit and decide to take the lighter path today. Wake up and appreciate yourself. Sing in the shower and uplift your spirits. Speak with an encouraging voice and don't criticise others. Remember to smile as much as you can (this will make you and everyone around you feel much better). Keep up this level of positive energy and you will notice that others will be more responsive than usual.

Today you have lifted your energy into a positive cycle and in doing so have created new choices for yourself. How does it feel?

*Choose to enjoy your destiny
every day.*

153

LEARN TO SURF

The truth is that stress is part of life; someone or something is always challenging us, but this doesn't mean we have to go down each time and become the victims of circumstance and other people's behaviour. You can negotiate the ups and downs by being true to yourself and being positive in your outlook and your actions; there is no need to get sucked under those waves when you can just ride them easily and effortlessly.

The way to keep focused and moving forward towards your objectives (regardless of the distractions and obstacles that you meet) is to take affirmative action towards your goals every day. Let positive action become an everyday habit for you and then – whatever life throws your way – you can still keep your eye on your target and move persistently towards it.

Try repeating the following positive affirmations; they will give you all the energy and bounce you need to surf the waves and stay on top (however bumpy the ride).

I deserve the best that life can give me.

Every day I move closer to my goals.

I know how to get what I want.

I trust myself.

I am a winner.

The universe supports my every move.

I am safe.

I create my own life.

☆ ☆ ☆

You can transcend your challenges.

154

OPEN YOUR HEART

Did you know that your heart will open if you:

Find something to appreciate. Put on your appreciative eyes and go out and look for something to be glad about. Keep looking until you feel your heartstrings tug. Some things you could look for: small flowers growing in the cracks in the pavement; a bird singing, just for the joy of it; a smile from a stranger; any act of kindness … leave your judgements behind; look for beauty and you will find it.

Tell someone how much he or she means to you. Write a letter; send an email; phone a friend; give someone a hug … give your love, with no strings attached and you will feel great.

Look into a mirror and say to yourself, 'I am good enough, just the way I am.'

This might make you cry (remember, this is also a sign that your heart has been moved).

Create something – a cake, a meal, a tidy room. Put a bunch of flowers on the table, light a candle. Give the project (however small) *all* of your attention. Someone once said that we are here to learn how to live and not how to win: feel glad, just to be alive.

Jump for joy, even if you have to pretend to feel joyful. Fake it until you make it. Jump as high as you can and shout, 'I love my life.' An emotional reaction is guaranteed (both laughter and tears are demonstrations of heart feelings).

Feel glad to be alive.

155

TRAIN UP YOUR MAN

Fed up with picking up his socks and putting down the toilet seat? Is there a grimy ring around the bath and wet towels on the bathroom floor? If you answer yes to any of these questions then I have to tell you that the fault is all yours.

We teach people how to treat us and how to act around us, so if you expect oafish behaviour from your man then that is exactly what you will get. Teach the man in your life how to become the partner you most want him to be (balanced, sensitive and housework-friendly). The training session must begin today.

Five tips for training up your man

1 If he's throwing underpants on the floor and drinking milk straight out of the carton these are signs that he still thinks he is living with his mum. Tactfully clarify the situation for him.

2 If he can clean his car then he can clean the house; gently point out that it takes exactly the same set of skills.

3 Appreciate, appreciate, appreciate (him). He will love this and will be much more amenable.

4 Continue to appreciate him in public; this builds a wonderful rapport. If you ever criticise your man in front of others you will never be able to get what you want; criticism is the biggest turn-off and damages intimate relationships.

5 Don't give up – domestic harmony leads to emotional harmony: a man with a mature attitude to household chores will also develop emotional maturity.

Perseverance furthers!

156

APPRECIATE YOUR WORTH

Your beliefs about yourself come true because you are always creating a self-fulfilling prophecy. So, for instance, if you undervalue yourself and expect to feel inferior then you will. And if you appreciate your worth and value your judgement then you will feel confident.

Think of a particular situation or area of your life where you feel low in confidence. Why do you feel like this? Your answers will demonstrate all sorts of 'evidence' that you have collected to 'prove' to yourself that you are: no good; can't do something; always mess up; can't take responsibility ... or whatever.

Now challenge this view. Think of times when you *have* shown the qualities that you think you lack. Collect all the evidence that you can to contradict your negative self-beliefs and *write it down*.

Ask the people who love you why they love you. Ask your close friends what they see in you. You will be amazed by what you hear.

You may have started to take your personal strengths and talents for granted – stop doing this! Add the positive opinions of others to your mounting list of evidence, which will confirm to you that you are a person of worth and ability.

Yes, you are worth it — every time!

157

STOP TRYING TO BE PERFECT

When it's totally perfect I will be content; when I lose more weight, then I will be happy; I must look absolutely right; everything must be totally together ... I must be Superwoman!

Do you recognise yourself here? Are you juggling career; partner; social life; family; children; plates; plates full of food; dirty clothes and anything and everything else, in a quest to become the most perfect woman you could ever wish to meet? Do you set yourself standards by which you judge the value of your days? Are you always striving to achieve more; do you ever give yourself a break? Try this quiz.

EXERCISE

Superwoman quiz

1 Friends are coming to dinner. Do you have to clean the house, cook something exotic and

complicated, and wear yourself out? Or do you take a more relaxed approach and expect your friends to take you as they find you and share a simple, easy-to-prepare meal?

2 You are feeling exhausted. Do you carry on regardless? Or do you give up and go to bed?

3 Do you think that you would be happier and more successful if you lost weight?

4 Do you feel incomplete if you aren't wearing make-up?

5 Do you sometimes push yourself beyond your limits?

6 Is it important to you that people think that you are always in control?

7 Do you ever feel that you are not good enough?

8 Would you describe yourself as a perfectionist?

Give yourself a break; you are 'good enough'.

158

CLEAN YOUR AURA

Have you ever met anyone and immediately felt the strength of their presence and personal power? We call this human quality *personal magnetism*, and indeed that is exactly what it is. Surrounding our physical body is a protective electromagnetic field that is created from our own radiations. We call this energy field the 'aura' and some people can see it as a halo of light. Most of us don't 'see' the aura but we can 'feel' it by being aware of it. Maybe you are aware of a greyness around a person who has just smoked a cigarette or a brightness around someone who is being positive. Our auras are absorbers of energy and soak up vibrations from *everything* around us. We need to keep our auras strong and clear so that we can maintain good health and strong positive energy.

Relax, close your eyes and become aware of the energy surrounding your body.

Imagine a halo of light surrounding you, following the contours of your body from the top of your head down one side and back up the other side of your body to your head again.

Follow this contour in your mind, visualising an unbroken line of light surrounding your whole body.

Now send a white beam of cleansing light around the contour of your aura. Imagine this light as a vacuum cleaner sucking out any dirt and negativity.

When your aura looks bright and clean open your eyes.

With your freshly cleansed aura you will feel like a million dollars.

159

GET BACK TO YOUR ROOTS

Many of us live a fast-paced lifestyle and it is so easy lose to our connection with our natural roots. One of the most effective ways to calm the mind and to centre ourselves is to get in touch with the natural world.

Plan to escape the town or city even if it can be for only a few hours a week. If this is impossible, then take a walk in the park. Take time to appreciate the wonders of nature: the colour of the sky, the green of the grass, the beauty of flowers, the songs of the birds.

Sometimes low spirits are just the result of trying too hard to keep up with the pressures and pace of modern life. So take a natural break and enjoy the simple pleasures and restore yourself and your happiness.

Get grounded

When you can't get out to enjoy the natural world, try this technique (you can do it while you are sitting at your desk or on the bus).

- Sit or stand with your feet apart, soles flat on the ground.
- Close your eyes.
- Become aware of the energy points at the centre of the soles of both your feet.
- Feel the gentle tugging of the earth.
- Visualise the connection. Imagine roots leading from these energy points, way down into the centre of the earth. You are connected!
- Feel that your energy is grounded, centred and focused.

Get connected to your natural roots.

160

USE YOUR ANGER

Act *out of* your anger and not *in* it. Remember the last time that you were really angry? How did you act? Did you behave assertively and resolve your feelings or did you just see red and say and do all the wrong things? In other words, did you act *out of* your anger or did you act *in* it?

EXERCISE

Your volcano of anger

We are often afraid of our anger because it is a powerful force. So, when the sparks are about to fly a mixture of emotions can confuse us, including resentment, hatred, guilt and fear. The next time this happens try the following four steps.

1 Accept your anger and allow yourself to feel it.
2 Recognise that this is your own powerful energy.
3 Visualise a volcano going off inside you, filling you with power and energy. Have the major

eruption inside of you rather than outside. In this way you can consciously use your anger rather than letting your anger use you.

4 This initial inner blast will clear your mind so that you can act and speak coherently and assertively.

Anger is a natural emotion that only becomes dangerous if we continue to deny it.

Act out of your anger (using your power constructively) rather than in your anger (going berserk) and there will be a dramatic change in the way that you feel.

161

INCREASE YOUR
SEX-ESTEEM

Self-confidence is the greatest aphrodisiac of all: when you know yourself and know what you want, you look and feel sexy. When you are feeling good you are looking good so build up your confidence and let it show in your posture and body language. Walk tall and hold your head high and look and act assertively. (This will soon become a habit even if it feels like you are faking it at first.)

The majority of people are dissatisfied with the way their bodies look; hence the massive growth in the diet and health and fitness industries.

Don't buy into a negative self-image cycle or it will ruin your happiness (and your sex life). The cycle goes like this: I hate the way my ... looks/if only I could lose weight/change my shape/look like ... I would be happy. I hate the way my... looks, etc. When you hate any part of your body and when you believe your happiness depends on physical changes, you are caught in a cycle of low self-esteem and low confidence. Step out of this cycle and release your inner sex goddess!

Stop trying to be physically perfect and learn to love your body, even if this seems impossible at first. Start by admiring a small piece of you (for example your fingernail) and then move on to cover the rest.

Be happy in your own skin
and your body confidence and
sex—esteem will hit the roof.

162

FOLLOW THROUGH

If you are known as a decisive go-getting sort of person then others will be inclined to take you and your plans more seriously – more seriously, that is, than they will take someone who dithers and twitters around in a whirlpool of uncertainty.

Just think how annoying it can be when you ask someone their opinion and they just can't come down on one side or the other. Of course they might just be 'keeping their options open', which I think is often only a polite way of saying that they can't commit. And here we get to the very heart of positive assertive action: to achieve your goal you must be committed and ready to make the decisions that will ultimately lead to your success. There are always the two choices:

1 NO COMMITMENT = NO RISK = NO DECISION = NO PLAN = NO GOAL

2 COMMITMENT = READY TO TAKE A
   CHANCE = DECISION = PLAN =
   GOAL

If you take choice number one you are choosing not to follow through, and this is OK as long as you are aware that you have made this choice. But if you do this unconsciously then you might think that things didn't come together because you are a victim of circumstance (things never go your way, you are a born loser, etc. etc.). If you are in any situation where you are feeling out of control and in a mess just check: did you take the first choice?

Commitment leads to success.

163

TAKE CONTROL OF YOUR LIFE

No, your life doesn't have to be a chaotic muddle from the moment you wake up to the moment you collapse into bed. You *can* relax and take control! All you need to do is run a 'Life Zone Check', to see where and what you might need to change.

Life Zone Checklist

Relationships:

Do your relationships support you?

Do you ever feel taken for granted?

Self-Image:

Are you positive and upbeat?

Are you self-confident?

Do you believe in yourself?

Health/Fitness:

Does your lifestyle support good health?

Are you getting enough exercise?

Do you look after yourself?

Are you high in body confidence?

Money:

Are you good at managing your money?

Do you ever spend more than you earn?

Do you need to earn more money?

Work:

Do you like the work that you do?

Is your job fulfilling?

Would you like a career change?

Spirituality:

Are you able to switch off from 'doing' and just 'be'?

Can you tap into your inner strength?

Do you believe that your contribution is important?

Decide to make the changes you need to make. Take charge of the way you run your life and you will feel in control.

You are in charge!

164

ALWAYS BE A WINNER

Confident people love life and they are brimming over with enthusiasm and positive expectation. This doesn't mean that they never have to face hard times or setbacks; it means that when they do they can call on their reserves of optimism, trust and buoyancy to keep them afloat. Being able to love your life means that you can appreciate your downs as well as your ups. Sounds crazy? Well, not really; it's the sanest way to live.

There are peaks and troughs in everyone's life and the trick is to learn how to surf the waves of both extremes. Each time you face a challenge and ride it out you will become stronger and more confident.

Think of a time when you have had to demonstrate your own powers of endurance, patience, tolerance or whatever in difficult circumstances. You come out of such times feeling a greater sense of self-respect and self-worth, don't you? But why wait to appreciate your gains until after you survive a bad patch? Confident people recognise that they are learning life's lessons all the time and that the sooner they learn from them the quicker they will be able to move onward and upward in their life. This attitude only requires a subtle shift in awareness that creates an all-win situation out of every circumstance.

Trust in the ultimate goodness
of the universe and you will
always be able to turn things
around to serve you.

165

STOP BEING A PEOPLE PLEASER

Life-changing decisions stir up the people who share your life and often this is why pessimists love to remain in the 'safe' prison of their victim status. At some point you have to be prepared to put your needs first and if you are over-concerned with pleasing others you will never get what you really want. And if you think that you have never been too nice for your own good then do this exercise and think again.

EXERCISE

People pleaser checklist

Answer the following questions to discover just how nice you are prepared to be.

- Do you ever feel taken for granted?
- Would you stay late at work when asked, even if you don't want to?

- Do you ever ask permission to speak or to act in a certain way?
- Do you often apologise for your behaviour?
- Are you ever worried about what others think?
- Do you ever think that some people are 'better' than you?
- Do you often use the word 'sorry'?
- Is it hard for you to say no to people?
- Do you often find yourself doing things that you really don't want to do?
- Do you ever not say what you really mean?

Whenever you feel your smile sticking to your face; whenever you are saying yes when you are longing to say no; when you are feeling used and are becoming resentful; when you feel angry with the world – it's time to stop being a people pleaser.

It's time to start pleasing yourself.

166

FORGIVE YOUR PARENTS

If you have a wonderful understanding with your parents then this may not seem relevant to you. However, most of us, at some time, will feel the need to clear up our relationship with our parents.

As we learn more about ourselves we understand the way that negative patterning is passed on from parent to child. There comes a time when we might start to recognise that many of our self-limiting beliefs were learned from our parents and from our childhood environment. We may then feel angry with our parents, thinking such things as:

> *'Why did my mother treat me like that? Why didn't my father show me that he loved me? Why did he hit me? Why did she let him treat me badly? Why did they always laugh at me? Why did they say I was stupid? Look how it ruined my confidence ...'*

You may have recognised some of your own negative behaviours, thoughts and feelings in your parents. As soon as you identify this patterning you are beginning a big change in your life. You cannot let go of negativity and replace it with positivity if you are still blaming your parents. Let go of whatever you think your parents 'did' to you. Seek professional help if you need it.

Remember, your parents did the best they could. We can only teach and pass on what we already know, and that is what they did.

Start to forgive your parents and you will start to feel like a new person.

167

RE-INVENT YOURSELF

One of the fantastic things about going on holiday is that because no one knows you, you can feel free to be different.

We can easily become reflections of what people expect of us and these expectations can lead us into staying the same: wearing the same type of clothes, looking the same, doing the same things, saying the same things. Our friends and loved ones can get alarmed when we behave out of character and so, if it gets too uncomfortable to make a change, we can easily slip back into our usual image.

You don't have to do anything too drastic to feel different. You can re-invent yourself. When we are feeling flat we usually fall into an easy habitual lifestyle, where we do what we always do. This might give temporary security but it does not give a buzz to our lives. Recharge your life by changing something about yourself – dare to be different.

Being different

Do something that is out of character. Here are a few ideas:

- How long have you had the same hairstyle? More than a year? Change it.

- Do you always wear flats? Wear a pair of heels.

- Find a new friend, someone who is quite unlike you.

- Start a new hobby/nightclass.

Begin with small changes and notice how you feel. If being different is difficult at first just keep on practising.

Change is like a breath of fresh air; enjoy the new perspectives it brings.

168

MANAGE YOUR TIME

If you lead a busy life and you don't organise your time, sooner or later your busyness will overwhelm you.

A client created a serious sleep problem for herself because she didn't manage her time effectively. She had three young children and worked full time and (in her words) 'just muddled along'. She came for coaching when she began waking up in a panic in the night and was unable to get back to sleep again. She traced the panic to a feeling of being 'out of control' of her life, and she spent her sleepless hours worrying about things she 'should' have done or 'must remember' to do. This is a common syndrome that easily develops as we take on more and more responsibilities. Happily there is an easy solution: time management.

Time management

1 Write things down, create lists of things to do, use a pinboard, use a diary.

2 Look at the lists, pinboard and diary!

3 Prioritise your jobs. Do you really need to do everything on your list? If not, delete those items.

4 Stop procrastinating – do the worst jobs of the day first. If you keep putting things off you will lose self-respect.

5 Say 'no' when you need to. Don't spend time worrying about how you are going to (eventually) back out.

6 Take time out for yourself in the spaces that you have created by good time management.

If your own time is valuable to you then start to manage it!

169

MAKE AN ACTION PLAN

Choose one of your short-term goals (achievable in three months or less). Take a piece of paper and divide it into five columns with the following headings.
INTENTION METHOD NEEDS REVIEW CHANGES

Fill in the columns in the following way
INTENTION:
State your goal. *I want to* ....

METHOD:
The specific action steps I need to take are (list these in order) ....

NEEDS:
List all the resources you may need: e.g. help, professional advice, family support. This list might alter as time passes.

REVIEW:
Give yourself some realistic deadlines.

Decide on certain dates to assess your progress.

CHANGES:
Note any changes that occur. This is your flexibility column and will affect the rest of your plan. Be ready to adapt your plan so that you can respond creatively to change instead of being floored by the first setback.

Once you have achieved a short-term goal you will be inspired to plan for more ambitious and far-reaching goals. You can use exactly the same procedure for a long-term goal. Let your plan be specific but also flexible (a focused and relaxed approach is the way to success). Tick off the action steps as you achieve them and make sure that you celebrate each and every positive step forward.

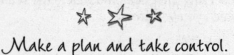

Make a plan and take control.

170

WATCH WHAT YOU ARE THINKING

Form follows thought. This means that whatever we create in our lives was once a thought. Your house was once a thought in an architect's mind; your dinner was a thought before you cooked it; this book was a thought before I wrote it. This is such an obvious idea and yet it has profound consequences.

Imagine your thoughts as magnets. As you send out your thoughts you are sending out magnets into the world. These magnets attract their duplicates in material form – *thoughts are things*, so watch what you are thinking. If, deep down, you can't believe that you deserve something then you can be sure that you will never get it; you are sending out 'not deserving' magnets and that is the reality which you will create.

Creating your heart's desire

Expand your thoughts by developing your imagination. Think of what you would most like to happen in your life. Concentrate on possibilities, think big, and change any negative expectations.

Write down all the things you would like to create. Be as clear and specific as you can.

Close your eyes and visualise your outcome; really feel and taste your success.

Keep playing with these ideas throughout the day. Have a strong, clear intention to get what you want. Focus on your outcome and this will eventually attract the ways and means of it into your life.

Watch your thoughts; make powerful positive affirmations; visualise these affirmations in action and consciously create your heart's desire.

171

APPRAISE YOUR RELATIONSHIP PROSPECTS

Intimate love relationships can work only when both partners have a strong sense of self-worth. If you enter a relationship in a vulnerable state (on the rebound/feeling needy) you will lack the confidence to be yourself and this will eventually lead to problems. Before you embark on a new relationship ask yourself the following questions:

Am I feeling needy?

Is this a good relationship choice?

Does he respect me?

Am I at ease with him or am I on edge?

Do I feel safe with him?

Is he trustworthy and reliable?

Do I respect him?

Is he needy?

What are his positive qualities?

What are his negative qualities?

Am I happy with myself?

Is he happy with himself?

Do I need to resolve any personal issues before I commit to a new relationship?

Consider your answers. What do they reveal about the possibilities for this relationship?

Be guided by your clear, cool appraisal.

172

GET BODY CONFIDENT

Body confidence is not dependent on how you look on the outside; it is all about how you feel about yourself on the inside. Try the following tips and get confident about the way you look.

Ten tips to create a positive self-image

1 Stop comparison shopping. When you compare yourself with others you will always feel intimidated.

2 Love and appreciate all that your body does for you. You are perfect just the way you are.

3 Celebrate your unique qualities and optimise your best features.

4 Always be a first-rate version of yourself rather than a second-rate version of someone else.

5 Look beyond the image in the mirror and see the talented and creative

woman that you are.

6 Enjoy the fantasy of glossy media hype but don't let impossible dreams steal your happiness.

7 Walk tall and carry yourself with pride; you will feel so much better about yourself.

8 Smile and the world smiles with you. Laugh more and you will look and feel great.

9 Keep your energy levels high by making sure that you eat well and take enough exercise. When your energy is buzzing and positive you look and feel wonderful.

10 A positive self-image attracts attention. Become an exciting and interesting person who glows with self-confidence and knows that there is much more to life than being a size ten!

Love the skin you are in.

173

REMEMBER: BE HERE NOW

It's Saturday morning, a day off, and time to go shopping. As you get in the car one of the children starts complaining, so you say, 'Be quiet, we have to go shopping.' Then the baby cries and you get more uptight. Your partner starts yelling and you shout, 'Oh, stop yelling – he's only a baby.' Things are becoming very tense ... STOP! Do you recognise this sort of scene?

Substitute any situation where your well-formed plans aren't working. Don't keep bashing on in the face of such resistance ... stop and recognise the moment. Consciously place yourself into the present moment.

Let go of thoughts about the past or the future and appreciate and act in the NOW.

If you become so organised and together that you are busy living in the future or you are rushing to keep track of time then you are missing the true pleasure of the moment and efficiency has cost you too much. Whenever you feel that your life is running out of control, stop and say to yourself, 'Remember, be here now!'

This doesn't mean that you have to let go of everything. Sort out the babies and *then* go shopping. If the telephone rings then answer it (it's happening in the moment). Make that appointment for three weeks' time (you make it in the moment and in three weeks' time you will keep the appointment in the moment).

The power is always in the moment.

Stop reading and recognise the moment; feel the now.

174

EXPECT THE BEST

Imagine that you have just woken up feeling low. 'Oh no,' you think, 'this is going to be a bad day.' You start the day expecting the worst to happen – and it will! Who wants to communicate with you in that mood? If anything good comes along you will miss it because you aren't expecting it and no one can be bothered to point it out to you. A negative attitude attracts negative people and events into your life.

Expect the worst to happen and it will; you will 'prove' your low expectations to be true.

Now, let's start all over again. You wake up feeling low but you know how to change your mood: 'I don't feel at my best but, still, I know it's going to be a good day.' And it will be. It will definitely be better than your first try. You smile and make the effort to lift your spirits, and those around you will respond to you. You are high in expectation, so when that great opportunity presents itself you will be able to recognise it and go for it!

But sometimes expecting the best can be harder to do when things are going well than when we are struggling with nothing to lose. So when the world is sweet, accept this and keep expecting it to be so. Don't start looking for possible problems and 'what ifs'. Just enjoy.

Let your optimistic genie out of the bottle and always expect the best.

175

SUFFER IN STYLE

The next time you are feeling fed up I want you to *really* feel fed up. This means that you don't just sit and moan and feel miserable but that you sit and close your eyes and feel your energy. This heavy, depressed feeling is your *energetic* response to whatever is going on. If you are enjoying your misery (and who doesn't enjoy a good wallow every now and again) then just get into your energy and stay with it for as long as you like.

Sometimes when I feel like this I tell my family that I'm disappearing for a while and that I'm going under the duvet. And I do just that. I get into bed, pull the duvet over my head and have a good old miserable time. And somehow this changes things as my energy shifts into an upward gear and I start to come out of my mood.

However, if you aren't in for a good energy slump (you are nowhere near your bed or you just want to feel better quickly), simply link with the power of your energy. Recognise that you can change your mood by lifting your awareness. Remember that you are part of the amazing flow of universal energy; see the bigger picture and leave your depressing mood behind. Say the following affirmation:

Universal energy flows through me

As you practise becoming aware of energy you will start to feel more lively and responsive.

Watch for changes in your life as your awareness develops and grows.

176

DON'T LET IT GET TO YOU

Ducks swim in water but they never get wet, hence that saying 'like water off a duck's back'. The duck lives in the water but doesn't get affected by it, and this is just the way you need to learn to live your life. Your reserves of confidence get lower when you allow yourself to become too affected and distracted by all that is happening around you.

EXERCISE

Stay calm

The next time you feel emotionally stretched ask yourself this question: *Why am I letting this get to me?*

Now imagine that duck swimming in the pond with the water droplets rolling off its waterproofed feathers. You can be just as unperturbed by the strong forces in your life.

Visualise the duck and say to yourself: *This is just like water off a duck's back to me.*

Cultivate an image of yourself as a person who can easily let things go. You don't sweat the small stuff and you don't let things get to you. You roll with the punches and have the self-confidence to know that nothing and no one has the power to disturb your life.

After you have done this a few times the image of the duck will be enough to get you back on course (with a smile on your face).

You can rise above all that life throws at you; you are big enough!

177

LET GO AND RELAX!

Learn to recognise the difference between achieving important goals and ruining your life (and the life of your loved ones) by pushing yourself beyond your limits.

Tune into your feelings and you will know when you have gone too far. When you are feeling stretched just stop and ask yourself, 'How important is this'? If you're not feeling good does it really matter if the floor is dirty? So you aren't looking your best, does this have to ruin your day?

Take a reality check. Why does your life have to stay on hold until you are the perfect weight; have the perfect qualifications; have the perfect relationship; live in the perfect house ...? Sometimes the risk of change feels so challenging that we will come up with anything to delay it. Just check that you aren't doing this.

Let go of the need to control everything. This is such a great tip! What a relief to put down all those burdens. Yes, you are not indispensable (the world will keep turning after you have gone). Feeling and looking in control can become an obsessive desire. Often we use the appearance of control in order to hide our vulnerability and hurt. You can start to let go mentally and physically in small ways; no need to get into a panic, just let go a bit at a time. This will become easier and easier, and so will your life!

It is safe for you to let go.

178

IDENTIFY AND ELIMINATE UNNECESSARY STRESSORS

A certain amount of stress encourages us to achieve and to be dynamic in our lives as we learn to overcome life's challenges. However, too much stress can cause exhaustion, depression, lethargy and even illness. We all react differently to situations. One woman's stress exhilarator ('yes, I *can* meet that deadline') is another woman's stress poison ('no, I'll never do it, it's all too much for me'). Identify the unnecessary harmful stress in your life and eliminate it.

EXERCISE

Dealing with stress

Make a list of all the things that are negatively stressful to you. Think carefully about each stressor. Can you let go of it, change it or accept it in some way? Make a table like the one shown and find a constructive approach to the elimination of unnecessary stress in your life.

Stressor I always feel lethargic.

Change Cut down on alcohol and junk food. Eat healthily and take more exercise.

Consequences Feel better. Look better. Feel more in control. Increased self-respect.

Stressor I'm always lookng for a man (woman)to make my life feel complete.

Let go Do without an intimate relationship for a while. Learn to get to know myself.

Consequences Increased self-esteem. I know that I am an interesting person and I don't have to depend on others for acceptance.

Stressor I hate .... (name of person)

Accept Forgive, accept and release this person from your angry thoughts.

Consequences Feeling of lightness and freedom as I release my anger and hatred.

Don't let stress get you down; face the issues and deal with them and you will feel so much better.

179

SAY 'NO' WHEN YOU WANT TO

'No' is such a small word but it is perhaps one of the hardest for us to use. A client once told me that she was ten years into her marriage before she could tell her husband that 'no' she didn't like having her hair stroked. When they first met her husband had loved to stroke her hair and he had asked her if she liked it too. She had said 'yes' when she really meant to say 'no' because she wanted to please him. It wasn't until after the birth of her third child that she told her husband her true feelings. He was astounded and amazed that she hadn't told him sooner.

If you are saying 'yes' when you really want to say 'no' then you are not being true to yourself and this will affect your feelings of self-respect. We all struggle with this little word as we find ourselves doing all sorts of things that we really don't want to do. If we don't say 'no' when we want to, we act with anger and resentment and our self-esteem takes a further nosedive.

EXERCISE

Practise saying 'no'

- Say it out loud when there's no one around, just to get used to saying it.

- Now imagine a situation where you would like to say it.

- See the person in your mind's eye and visualise yourself saying 'no' to them.

- When you feel ready do it for real!

Keep practising this — it gets easier and easier.

180

KNOW YOUR WORTH

EXERCISE

I am ....

Look at this list. Which phrases do you think describe you best? Which phrases would you say least describe you?

- Thoughtful and kind.
- Deserving the best that life can offer.
- Able to express my feelings.
- Not good enough at certain things.
- Boring.
- Able to tackle new projects.
- Creative.
- Inclined to give up easily.
- Able to communicate well with others.
- Good at coping with any situation.
- Basically a lazy person.

- Articulate and clever.

- Well-motivated and energetic.

- Good at making decisions.

- Interesting.

- Not really good at anything in particular.

Consider your answers. Do your beliefs about yourself serve to increase or decrease your feelings of self-worth? Look closely at any beliefs that have a negative effect on your life – are they actually true?

For who or what are you not quite good enough? Give up this negativity; you are good enough!

181

LOVE AND VALUE YOURSELF

Deep down we are all excessively self-critical, even the seemingly most confident people have a well-developed 'inner critic'. The inner critic is that part of each of us which nags away and is *never* satisfied with our performance. You can easily recognise its voice: it is the one that tells you off all the time; the one that keeps saying that you are never good enough/clever enough/thin enough/educated enough to do or be anything of note in this world. It is important to understand that the inner critic will never be content because its work is never over – its job is to keep on criticising and so it always keeps us on the hook.

Deal with your inner critic

Accept that the inner critic will go on nagging at you.

Learn to recognise the voice of your inner critic. As soon as you start to feel low, listen to what you are saying to yourself. Are these negative things really true or is this the voice of your inner critic?

Visualise your inner critic resting in a deckchair, drink in hand, feet up in some exotic location. In other words, send your inner critic on holiday, keep him/her happy and he/she will stop telling you off.

Work on your inner critic and soon you won't be continually bringing yourself down. You are an incredible and multi-talented person.

Love and value yourself, be your own best friend; this relationship will last forever.

182

REAP WHAT YOU SOW

Because our energy is magnetic we will draw to ourselves the type of energy that we project. The modern interpretation of this is, 'What goes around comes around.' We can all remember experiences where we have very clearly reaped what we have sown. I have always been fascinated by this notion and although I have recognised the truth and fairness of it as it has appeared in my life, I have never fully understood the mechanics behind the wisdom until fairly recently.

In practice, this principle demonstrates that all those things we think about most strongly, all those beliefs and expectations we hold and the strength and power of our imagination come together and attract into our lives exactly what we are giving out. We do indeed attract what we radiate.

Think of a difficult time when you were not full of aliveness and energy and recollect the progress of events. When we are faced with great challenges we often become fearful and anxious and this is, of course, a natural reaction. As we become less open to the positive life force we start to feel depressed and our energy levels fall. This negative state tends to attract all the frightening possibilities that are filling our thoughts and so we create a familiar, negative self-fulfilling prophecy, *'I told you so, I knew it would all turn out badly, you see I was right all along.'* Similarly, when we adopt a positive attitude we radiate expectations of success, happiness and support.

Radiate positivity and attract
the good into your life.

183

LOOK BEYOND YOUR IMAGE

Extricate yourself from the madness of a relentless pursuit of what our society deems to be the perfect body and face (you will always fail to deliver). A stick of mascara or even a new dress will not make you feel complete and happy; those feelings come from within.

Try focusing on something much more meaningful. For example, rather than asking, 'Why have I got cellulite?', you could ask, 'What is the real meaning of my life?' Put the focus of your attention where it will bring positive life-affirming results. Get things back into perspective by answering the following questions.

EXERCISE

Getting things in perspective

- Who are the people you love most in the entire world?

- What quality do you most admire in yourself?

- If you had only one week to live what would you say to whom?

- What would you love to accomplish?

- Are you afraid to take chances?

- What values are most important to you?

- Do you believe in yourself?

- What is your most wonderful achievement?

- Do you love life?

- What holds you back?

Think about your answers over the coming weeks. When you find yourself preoccupied with minutiae (sagging body parts, a broken nail, a bad hair day) lift yourself up and take a larger perspective. You are here to make the very best of your life by realising your full potential so make your contribution count.

Remember that the quality of your life is more important than the way you look.

184

BRING YOUR SKELETONS OUT OF THE CLOSET

One of the most important things that happen to people who come on my workshops is that they realise that we all have what we consider to be shameful secrets. You are not alone, everyone has thought and done things that they wished they hadn't, and we all make mistakes. But if you have hidden these things away you are also carrying a burden of guilt and shame as well as fear (that they will be revealed). Open the closet. I'm not suggesting that you reveal all on national TV or even that you tell anyone. Just take a look at these things on your own and as you look at them they lose their mystery and power:

Yes, I did this, I've paid my price in guilt and now I can let go of it. And yes, I said that and it had a terrible effect. Maybe I could apologise to that person or just let it go; I have punished myself enough.

Reviewing your skeletons

If your closet is full of rattling, secret skeletons then
you are using up a lot of energy in just trying to
keep that closet door shut (what if they should all
come bursting out?) Take the following steps:

- Invite them out for an airing.

- Survey each one coolly.

- Remedy anything that you can.

- Let them rattle off in peace.

*Let go of your guilt and you
will feel your energy increase
dramatically.*

185

BALANCE YOURSELF

When we are feeling high in self-esteem our mind, body, spirit and emotions are balanced. If our lives become out of balance in some way then our self-esteem will fall apart.

If, for example, I spend the whole day writing this book (mental activity), then by bedtime I will be wound up and feeling physically uncomfortable. If I spend the whole day analysing my feelings about having to get the book finished (emotional activity), then there will have been no action and no writing, and I will be panicking at bedtime! I could spend the whole day walking (physical activity), good exercise if I need it and have no deadline to meet. However, if I walk all day none of the job will be done and I will be anxious. I could meditate and visualise the book being written in time (spiritual activity), a good tactic but not on its own – it needs to be supported by real action.

We are built for mental, physical, emotional and spiritual activities. If you are feeling less than your best, check to see if you are in balance by answering the following questions:

◆ How much mental activity have I had today?

◆ How much physical activity have I had today?

◆ How long have I been in touch with my emotions today?

◆ How much spiritual activity have I had today?

When your life is balanced you will feel high in self-esteem and full of vigour.

186

DITCH YOUR WORRIES AND SEEK PLEASURE

Do you ever feel weighed down by your problems? Of course you do. We are inclined to carry around our worries and negative thoughts as if they were some important baggage that we dare not put down.

EXERCISE

Leaving that useless baggage behind

Whenever you feel tense and your mind is full of concern, stop for a moment, wherever you are.

1 Visualise yourself holding large, heavy suitcases full of your negative emotions (no wonder you feel so drained).

2 Put them down on the ground.

3 Now see yourself walking away from them.

4 Leave your worries behind you; they can wreck your life.

Now you have cleared up your energy and you are

free to welcome pleasure into your life. Would you describe yourself as a pleasure seeker or are you waiting for enjoyment to come and knock at your door? It won't – you have to go out and look for it.

- Focus on whatever makes your heart sing and puts a spring in your step.

- Recognise these experiences and nurture them.

- Stay away from moaners and worriers.

- Surround yourself with pleasure seekers.

- Know how to create enjoyment and then you can do this whenever you wish.

Expect pleasure and seek pleasure, and you will find it.

187

BE HAPPY TO BE YOURSELF

Know that you are special. Stop comparison shopping and start living by your own lights. Control your natural desire to compare yourself with others; the important thing to remember is that you are good enough, just the way you are. There is no need to try to become someone else; you are unique and special, just believe this to be true.

Repeat the following mantra: *I am happy to be me.* Say it, sing it, shout it, write it, as many times a day as you can. Your sense of inner strength and self-belief will increase and you will begin to let go of the need to compete.

Allow yourself to *be* yourself. Don't waste your life trying to be Superwoman or some other mythical creature who is more talented / more beautiful / more deserving than you! Drop those defences and accept the real you: she is fabulous, talented and truly amazing!

Enjoy yourself. All this competition entering has made us very worried bunnies (with such important concerns as: *Does my bum look too big in this? Am I too fat to wear a swimming costume? Is this piece of work really good enough or do I need to go over and over it just in case …? Does he think that I'm boring and uninteresting? How can I ever look as beautiful as Catherine Zeta Jones?*). Imagine giving advice to a grown-up daughter; now give that advice to yourself.

Learn to be yourself.

188

PROJECT A POSITIVE
SELF-IMAGE

What sort of person do you think you are? If I asked you to choose your top ten adjectives to describe yourself, what would they be? Write them down and see what you come up with.

Are you creative, friendly, kind, tolerant, generous, skilful, talented, sensitive, articulate and intelligent?

Are you boring, lazy, fearful, troubled, shy, controlling, critical, miserable, passive and untalented?

Your list is probably a mixture of negative and positive characteristics. The words that you use to describe yourself create your self-image – the impression that you present to the rest of the world. Are you creating the right impression? If your self-image is positive and assertive, others will see and feel your confidence and will show you the respect that you deserve. But if your self-image is negative you will come over as a person who is lacking in confidence and this will affect the way that others treat you.

If your list contains any negative characteristics, delete them. Create a list of positive qualities and start to project them into your life: live them and become them!

Take any negatives on your list and 'act as if' the opposite was true. For example if you think you are boring then decide to act as if you are fascinating. Get out there and fake it until you make it! And make it you will, because as you project your new image so you will become it.

Don't ever believe the least of yourself, you are so much more than you think you are.

189

HOLD THE BIGGEST THOUGHT

Relax, close your eyes and visualise a beautiful pond. Perhaps it has bulrushes; maybe you can hear frogs croaking; are there dragonflies swooping across the surface? The sun is shining in a cloudless, blue sky. Absorb the details, set the scene and then you can recreate it at any time.

See yourself at the edge of the pond, looking and feeling confident. You bend down and pick up two smooth grey pebbles; one is much larger than the other. As you hold one in each hand you can feel the difference in weight between the two; notice which hand holds which pebble.

Now throw the pebbles into different parts of the pond. As you watch, you see the circle of small ripples made by the lighter stone and the larger circle of ripples made by the heavier stone. You watch as the larger waves overcome the smaller ones *and you know that*, in just the same way, the positive thought you hold is big enough to overwhelm your smaller and limiting beliefs.

After you have done this visualisation a number of times you will reach a stage where you see yourself only throwing in a large pebble. This action symbolises your desire to only think the biggest, highest and most positive thought.

Hold the biggest thought and you will be amazed at the way life starts to treat you.

190

CHANGE YOUR RELATIONSHIPS

Men marry women and expect that they will always stay the same and women marry men thinking that they will change them! We are from different planets, there is no doubt. But whether you are on Mars, Venus or Earth the same truth prevails: you can only ever change yourself. And this is the magic key to creating amazing relationships. The ways that people react towards you are a reflection of the ways that you feel about yourself. It works like this:

THE WAY YOU FEEL ABOUT YOURSELF	THE WAY OTHERS REACT TO YOU
High in self-esteem	Respectfully
Angry	With hostility
Judgemental	Critically
Low self-belief	With lack of trust
Positive	Responsive and receptive
Content and at peace	Harmoniously

Body confident, and attractive	With interest, drawn towards you
Negative	Bored, unsympathetic
Guilty	Blaming
Loving	Kind and caring

If you respect yourself then others pick up on your feelings and treat you with the respect you deserve. If you love and value yourself you will attract similar qualities from others. And if you think badly of yourself and are self-critical then others will reflect those feelings back to you. If you are low in confidence you will soon be able to convince everyone that you are no good, useless, pathetic ... etc. And if you blame yourself, well soon enough everyone will be holding you responsible for your inadequacies.

All of your relationships are a
reflection of the relationship
you are having with yourself.

191

DE-CLUTTER YOUR LIFE

The only way to approach this is easily, slowly and methodically. Go from room to room and write down the specific areas that need clearing. Whatever you do don't allow yourself to become overwhelmed by it all so that you give up before you start. Plan your de-junking campaign realistically, do one small job at a time and then cross it off your list.

EXERCISE

Use it or lose it

This isn't as drastic as it sounds because there really are three 'use it' categories: the useful, the beautiful and the sentimental. Collect some cardboard boxes and begin! As you evaluate each article ask yourself these questions.

Is it beautiful?

Is it useful?

Does it have sentimental value?

The first two are easy to decide but watch this last one. Are you sure you absolutely can't live without this item or is this nostalgic streak the very one that is creating your clutter problems? Be ruthless and decisive or you will never get to lose anything. And don't sabotage yourself by tackling too much at once so that you bury yourself in 'stuff' and end up just throwing it all back into new piles.

Once you have cleared an area, stop, rest and then do some more another day. Gradually you will fill boxes for the rubbish dump or for recycling and maybe for the charity shop. Pass things on to people who will appreciate them and use them.

As you begin to create new space around you your self-respect will reach dizzying heights.

192

BE AN ENCOURAGER

Who do you know who could do with some encouragement right now? Maybe it's you. One of the surest ways to give yourself hope is to inspire someone else. People have good intentions, they want to communicate and they want to be creative. These qualities may not always be obvious but be assured that they are always there (however deeply buried). So how can you be an encourager? Think of someone who encouraged you. What did they say? What did they do? The following exercise might help you with some ideas.

EXERCISE

How were you inspired?

1 Think of someone who encouraged and helped you to do your best. Write their name.

....

2 How did they inspire you? What did they do to help you to succeed?

....

3 How can you use these strategies to
   encourage someone else?

....

Look around you and find someone who needs
some inspiration. Demonstrate your belief in them
as this will increase their own confidence and self-
belief. Encourage them to take a positive approach
by looking at what they *can* do, rather than thinking
about what they can't do. Help them to focus on
their goal and to create an easy step-by-step action
plan. Sometimes a simple supportive reminder such
as 'you can do it' is enough to encourage others to
face their fears and move on.

*When you start to encourage
another person something
incredible happens — you feel
encouraged yourself.*

193

FOCUS ON YOUR STRENGTHS

When we are feeling low in self-esteem we can only see our weaknesses; if we make a mistake it just 'proves' how stupid and useless we are. There seems to be a natural tendency for us to bring ourselves down rather than to lift ourselves up. Perhaps we have been taught not to 'brag' about ourselves and not to 'show off' but to be modest. Personal levels of self-esteem *never* depend on what other people are thinking. Self-esteem depends only upon what we think about ourselves, and so if we bring ourselves down then that is exactly where we will stay – down!

We need to build ourselves up. This doesn't mean bragging and showing off, it means being quietly assertive. We all have weaknesses, but we can only change if we feel motivated and energetic. Negativity breeds depression and low energy levels. Positivity brings interest, motivation and the power to make changes. Forget about false modesty. Look to your strengths. What are you good at? These things can be big or small, it doesn't matter.

EXERCISE

Look to your strengths

When you are low in self-esteem, lift yourself out of depression by focusing on your strengths. Make a list of them.

  MY STRENGTHS ARE

. . . .

. . . .

. . . .

Write down as many as you can think of. Read them out loud. Be proud of your abilities.

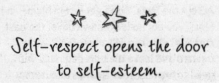

*Self-respect opens the door
to self-esteem.*

393

194

BE FORGIVING

Any old hurts, angers and hatreds that you carry for others just sit in your energy field attracting more of the same. Thoughts are magnets and as we send out negative energy we create a pathway for it to return to us; a fantastic reason to get to grips with forgiveness.

EXERCISE

Four steps to forgiveness

1 **State the facts.** View whatever happened as objectively as possible. Write down the facts and stick to the reality (don't embroider it with your emotions). So, for example, you might have written, *my mother was an alcoholic when I was growing up.*

2 **Accept the facts.** Don't get lost in blame and tears; you are no longer a victim of the past. A creative response will allow you to move forward and leave the hurt behind. If you need to express your feelings about what happened then make sure you do so, but

don't get stuck going over and over the same issue.

3 **Decide to let go.** Are you ready to let go or are you still gaining more from moaning, blaming and complaining? Sometimes it's only possible to forgive a bit at a time. (I can forgive this but not *that* at the moment.) Give yourself time and take it one step at a time.

4 **Enjoy the freedom** that your forgiveness brings. The more you can forgive, the lighter you will feel, as you free up your energy for more positive use.

Forgiveness is a process that heals the wounds of the past.

195

VISUALISE A CONFIDENT YOU

Think of a time when you let yourself down in some way. What aspects of your self-image were you projecting? Don't go down a self-critical path here, just remain detached and think realistically.

Still with this air of detachment, think of the ways that you could have supported yourself in this situation. What positive qualities would you have needed to project?

Now close your eyes and slow down your breathing. When you are feeling physically and mentally relaxed, enjoy the following visualisation.

Confidence visualisation

Imagine that you have all the positive characteristics that you need to be true to yourself in any situation that you might meet. Take these qualities one at a time and 'see' yourself projecting them out into the world. Feel what it would be like to be confident, assertive, capable, intelligent, creative ... etc.

Return to your original situation and *see* and *feel* the positive elements of your self-image that would have allowed you to be true to yourself in the circumstances. Get right into the skin of these positive aspects and know exactly how it feels to deal confidently and creatively with this situation.

When you are ready, open your eyes and come back into the room.

Now you know how to simulate the exact feelings that go with your positive self-image and you can easily project them into real-life scenarios. The next time you are faced with a similar situation you will know exactly how to deal with it.

You can project all the confidence that you need.

196

CREATE A NEW REALITY

Choose your goal and *write it down* – this physical action helps to make it real. Make sure that you believe that your objective is achievable in the fairly near future. (Don't try long-term aspirations until you are confident in the process.)

EXERCISE

Visualise your goal

- Go into a state of relaxation and tune into your imagination.

- See your wish come true. Put yourself at the very centre of the scene, see the detail, hear the sound effects, feel the appropriate emotions, tap into the heightened energy, bring the setting alive and make it feel real: live the dream now.

- When you feel the 'aliveness' recede, the visualisation has ended.

Focus on your new pictures throughout the day, and let the new reality become a part of your everyday consciousness. Remember to energise your goal with strong and appropriate positive affirmations (e.g. *I am a success; I am confident; I have a terrific new job; I own my dream car; my relationships support me; I am healthy; I love my life ... etc*).

Do this for a week, devoting at least fifteen minutes a day to your relaxed-state visualisation. Support this by daily focus as you go about your business and ensure that your thoughts (affirmations) match your pictures. Reflect upon your situation at the end of the week. What has changed? Look carefully with your inner eyes – the change might be subtle but it will be there.

Visualise, focus and affirm and make your dreams come true.

197

MAKE TIME FOR THE THINGS YOU LOVE

Are you managing your time efficiently and happily? Are you able to make time for the things you love to do?

EXERCISE

Dividing your time

1 Look at how you use your time. Draw a circle about six inches in diameter. Think about the way your time is used in different activities and divide up your 'pie'. This is your 'time used' pie chart.

TIME USED

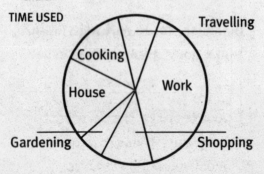

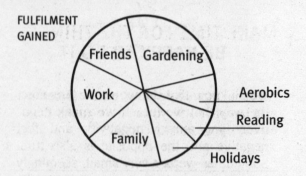

FULFILMENT
GAINED

Friends
Gardening
Work
Aerobics
Reading
Family
Holidays

2 Now put this chart aside. Using another piece
   of paper draw another circle to represent those
   activities where you gain most fulfilment. Don't
   look at the first chart while you are drawing the
   second one.

3 Put the charts side by side. What are the
   differences between the two? How could you
   manage your time to allow for more personal
   satisfaction?

Learn to make the very best
use of your time; it is your
most valuable resource.

198

BE HAPPY TO DO IT

We all know that the words we use affect the way that we feel. If we speak negatively we attract negativity and feel negative and the opposite is also true. Sometimes we use very small, seemingly innocuous words that can dramatically affect the quality of our lives.

Recently I rang the information desk of a large company and the lady on the telephone was really helpful. Each time I asked her a question she said that she would find out but that she had 'got to' look at the database/ask a colleague/look up further details. She used the term 'got to' five times in five minutes. Now imagine that she is answering that busy helpline for eight hours a day and every minute she says 'I've got to ...' – that's 480 'got tos' in one working day.

When we think we have 'got to' do something we put ourselves under pressure – just notice how you are feeling when you use that phrase. Well, after listening to this lady I became alerted to the potential power of 'got to' to ruin my day and I began to notice every time I said it.

Every time I was about to say 'got to' I replaced it with 'I'll be happy to …' This little trick works like magic. Why shouldn't we be happy doing even the simplest of things?

Watch your words and start to get happy to do things and before you know it you will be feeling happy.

199

NEVER *EVER* GIVE UP

When your life is hard and difficulties seem to appear whichever way you turn it is natural to feel dejected. When we are in the midst of a trauma we will not feel inclined to take helpful advice on how to 'feel better'. At this stage we really need to experience the power of our feelings of sadness, grief, anger, rage, hurt, shame or whatever other strong emotion we are feeling.

However, the good news is that this immediate painful stage will pass. Everything changes, including our emotions. Remember that this is true and wait for that moment when your deep negativity begins to change. You might have been feeling very low for some time and then, one day, you sense a seed of hope.

A client whose husband had died was very depressed for a couple of years. She said that she just felt that her life was meaningless and that she could never feel enthusiastic about anything.

She dragged herself through her days and then one day in October she went to her grandson's Harvest Festival celebrations at school. A very small girl with flowers in her hair sang the first verse of 'All Things Bright and Beautiful' and this lady said that it felt as though her heart moved. The little girl rekindled a spark of joy and hope, and a healing process began.

The darkest hour is truly just before the dawn. Believe in the goodness of the universe and know that you can and will feel hopeful again.

200

BE YOUR BEST

You are amazing! This is the truth about you, so go out there and tell it, feel it, and live it. The woman who smiles back at you from the mirror knows her true worth and she expresses it in every moment of her life.

Love her for her grit and determination and her resilience in the face of sometimes overwhelming odds. Admire her style and grace when the chips are down and she is negotiating her future. Respect her flexibility and creativity as she hurdles her challenges. Comfort her when she is down and marvel at the way she rises up and bounces back *yet again*! No, you can't keep a good woman down; she is always moving onwards and upwards in pursuit of her dreams.

You have the energy and willpower to push towards your goals and this sense of direction and purpose will make you feel like a winner every time. What more can you ever do than to have a go and do your best? And when things don't always turn out the way you had hoped, you are safe and secure in the knowledge that you gave it your best shot; this is what is meant by a winning mentality.

◆ Let nothing grind you down.
◆ Let no one diminish you.
◆ Believe in yourself and know that you are here to do great things.
◆ And get out there and do them!

Touch others with your boundless optimism; positive energy is the greatest gift you can share with anyone.

Also by Lynda Field and available
from Vermilion

60 WAYS TO CHANGE YOUR LIFE

Lynda Field

Are you stuck in a routine or feel the need to make a fresh start? Then this little book will inspire you to embrace change and face life with a positive attitude. It will help you take control of your destiny and change your life for the better – forever.

60 WAYS TO FEEL AMAZING

Lynda Field

This little book is positively brimming with ways to bring positive energy into your life.

Try these simple and effective tips for your body and soul and you will discover how to feel amazing throughout the day, throughout your life.

365 INSPIRATIONS FOR A GREAT LIFE

Lynda Field

In this great guide by bestselling author Lynda Field, you will find 365 ways to make your own life fantastic. Read this book and discover:

- Inspirations for enjoying every moment of every day
- Inspirations for feeling sexy and strong
- Insp for lifting you up when you g down
- Insp for staying cool and cal
- Insp for shaping your future

Practica and vital, *365 Inspirations for a Great Life* shows you how you can make every day count, starting now.

WEEKEND LIFE COACH
How to Get the Life You Want in 48 Hours

Lynda Field

As Britain's most popular life coach, Lynda Field knows that change is easy when we can unwind and focus on our own needs, dreams and goals. In her experience, we can make the most progress when we are relaxed and calm, and therefore most able to make full use of her special no pressure/ high enjoyment approach.

This unique book will show you how to:
- Be more confident
- Look wonderful
- Have great relationships
- Make a new career move
- Increase your finances
- Just be happy in your own skin

Fun and full of brilliant ideas, *Weekend Life Coach* will re-motivate and inspire you to step into a fabulous new life – this coming Saturday and Sunday...

WEEKEND CONFIDENCE COACH
How to Kick the Self-Doubt Habit in 48 Hours

Lynda Field

If your confidence is at rock bottom, or you're plagued by self-doubt, give yourself the help of Lynda Field's hugely supportive, upbeat and motivating book.

In just 48 hours, you will learn the six important steps you need to kick the low-confidence habit and reach beyond your self-limiting beliefs to realise your true potential – in a way that will last for the rest of your life.

'Lynda's boosts can be done anytime, anywhere, and are easy to remember'

Top Sante

BE YOURSELF

How to Relax and Take Control of Your Life

Lynda Field

'Take control of your life and improve your self-confidence with the help of this encouraging book' *Here's Health*

Bestselling author Lynda Field explains that to lead a meaningful and happy life, we have to develop our inner strengths and balance our 'doing' with our 'being'.

This inspirational book is full of practical strategies for anyone who wants to be successful and happy without struggle, strain and stress – and find the heart of themselves at the same time.

'Inspiring' *Woman's Way*

Buy Vermilion Books

Order further Vermilion titles from your local bookshop or have them delivered direct to your door by Bookpost.

Also available by Lynda Field:

☐ 365 Inspirations for a Great Life	9780091887575	£4.99
☐ Weekend Life Coach	9780091894689	£7.99
☐ Weekend Confidence Coach	9780091906870	£8.99
☐ Be Yourself	9780091887537	£7.99

FREE POST AND PACKING
Overseas customers allow £2.00 per paperback

Order
By phone: 01624 677237
By post: Random House Books
c/o Bookpost
PO Box 29
Douglas
Isle of Man, IM99 1BQ

By fax: 01624 670923

By email: bookshop@enterprise.net

Cheques (payable to Bookpost) and credit cards accepted

Prices and availability subject to change without notice. Allow 28 days for delivery. When placing your order, please mention if you do not wish to receive any additional information.

www.randomhouse.co.uk